WHY NOT YOU?

WHY NOT YOU?

An Accidental Entrepreneur's
Guide to Success

Amanda McKinney

NEW DEGREE PRESS

COPYRIGHT © 2023 AMANDA MCKINNEY

WHY NOT YOU?

An Accidental Entrepreneur's Guide to Success

ISBN

979-8-88926-918-2   *Paperback*

979-8-88926-961-8   *Ebook*

For you, the Accidental Entrepreneur with the courage to build a business on your terms. Every word is written for you.

CONTENTS

———

INTRODUCTION

.

___

The first time I ever visited New York City, I went with three girlfriends, and even though we were on the tightest college budget possible, we were rich in excitement on that trip and created many memories. But it actually wasn't the girl-time that made a lasting impression; it was the city. I fell in love with New York City on that first trip, like many people do.

As I was preparing to travel, I remember people telling me, "Don't look up, you'll look like a tourist." I'm sure these were words meant to keep me safe as a female going into the "big city," but to me it meant "don't look like you don't belong."

This small-town girl from Florida did *not* want to look like the small-town girl from Florida. I wanted to look like I belonged, like I had been there forever, like it wasn't new and exciting. I wanted to fit in and already know everything.

Well, guess what? This small-town girl looked up so fast I could have been wearing a flashing neon sign with the words

"Hey—I'm not from here!" And you know what, I'm glad I did because had I succeeded in fast-forwarding past the tourist part, I would have missed out on that memory and so many more.

I likely wouldn't have gone to Radio City Music Hall to take a picture of its iconic sign or snapped pics of the Statue of Liberty or wandered around Central Park watching others go about their day and making up stories about what their lives were like. I likely wouldn't have looked up to see the incredible skyscrapers that were so tall I couldn't believe my eyes.

Sure, I would have "fit in" more, but I would have missed that moment completely. And all the moments that followed during that trip.

And just like I wanted to fast-forward to not looking like a tourist, I bet you're trying to fast-forward through something right now too. You're likely testing business ideas, feeling all the feelings, and wishing more than anything else that you could be five years down the road.

I know this because not only was I in this exact place several years ago when I started my business, but any time I talk to new entrepreneurs, they all have something in common… they want to be further down the road in their journey. This is because most of us have discomfort when it comes to being a beginner.

For most of us, the beginner stage is something to be gone through as quickly as possible, like a socially awkward skin condition. But even if we're only passing through, we should pay particular attention to this moment. For once it goes, it's hard to get back (Vanderbilt 2021).

I challenge you to be fully present during your entrepreneurship journey. Instead of running as fast as you can to get further down the path, I would like to suggest that you stop and look up, just like I did at the skyscrapers in New York City.

Be in awe of where you are today.

In a few years, you will wish you had paused in this moment, no matter what moment this is for you. You can't ever go back, so take it in while you can because it's a beautiful place to be. And the good news is that you won't be in this moment too long, so take in the sights, enjoy them, and then move forward with intention.

CONGRATS, YOU'RE AN ACCIDENTAL ENTREPRENEUR!

If you and I were chatting over coffee (or tea, or wine, pick your fave; I like them all), and I asked you what title you would give yourself, you might not choose "entrepreneur." You might consider yourself a hobbyist turned "I think I could make money with this" or a stay-at-home parent looking to create cash flow for the family, or maybe everyone keeps telling you, "You could charge for this." Regardless, you're in the right place, and I'm talking to you in this book.

While you ultimately get to pick the title that resonates with you (CEO, founder, badass boss, etc.), for the purpose of this book, I've got a new title for you... Accidental Entrepreneur.

Here's my definition:

An Accidental Entrepreneur is anyone who stumbles into starting a business by following a passion or hobby. They are generally unsure that they qualify to run a business because they didn't go to business school and tend to want more education and training so they can "earn" the title. "Accidental" describes how they arrived at entrepreneurship but not how they will navigate through it because they want to intentionally create a business that integrates into their life instead of taking it over.

Hey there, Accidental Entrepreneur!

(Because I know you just said, "Yep! That's me!")

The cool part about adding the word accidental is that it automatically takes some of the pressure off. When something is accidental, it means that something occurred unexpectedly, and when this happens everyone knows being a little thrown off for a bit is okay, so you get a grace period.

You trip by accident; you have time to get up and get your footing.

You take a wrong turn by accident; you pause to let the GPS recalibrate.

So now that you have this new title of Accidental Entrepreneur, you can give yourself some grace and time to find your footing, and that's exactly what we're going to explore in this book:

CREATING A STRONG FOUNDATION, SO YOU CAN UNAPOLOGETICALLY CHASE YOUR DEFINITION OF SUCCESS

This book is filled with examples to inspire you as I know the benefit of reading actual examples. Specific sections to help you take action are also included in each chapter because inspiration is great, but action is what leads to more confidence as an Accidental Entrepreneur. Here's what you can expect in each chapter:

- Additional resources—shaded boxes are included within the text when there are references to checklists, timelines, podcast episodes, and other resources to help you with that topic.

- Key takeaways—a bulleted list to reiterate the main points of the chapter.

- Recommended actions—a numbered list of steps I recommend you take before moving on to the next chapter.

The other main component included is encouragement. My clients tell me often that I have a gift for helping people believe in themselves, and I'm honored to be able to encourage you through my words in this book. One way I want to do this is by letting you know that you're not alone in this bumpy road of entrepreneurship.

YOU'RE NOT ALONE

Now that you've slipped on the entrepreneur party hat, it's time to know who you're partying with. There are 528 million entrepreneurs in the world (Global Entrepreneurship Monitor 2023). And in 2022 alone, 5 million businesses were started (Commerce Institute 2023).

The pandemic certainly influenced the increase in businesses created as many people began thinking outside their traditional career options. In addition, there were new needs that had to be met, and that is the perfect opportunity for new entrepreneurs to emerge even if it wasn't their goal, hence the term Accidental Entrepreneur.

Whenever an influx like this comes about, it also comes with an influx of advice. On one hand this is a great thing because there's information at our fingertips, but on the other hand, we are met with a lot of advice that might not fit our needs.

Just like when you tell friends and family that you're going to visit a new place, if they have been there (or seen something on TV) they will share recommendations with you. Recommendations can lead you into the best restaurant in the city, but if someone recommends an Italian restaurant and you don't like Italian food, that's not going to be best for you.

To find your footing as an Accidental Entrepreneur, you have to do one thing that will make all the difference in the world, and it's to look inward, which is possibly the last thing your brain will be telling you to do. If you're anything like me, you will look everywhere else first. You'll read the books (thank you!), you'll listen to the podcasts, you'll buy digital courses and templates, but the best thing you can do is to look inward and ask questions.

Sure, there will be some questions you can't answer by going inward like "how to fix this dang internet issue," but to set a strong foundation for your business, you already have the answers inside you. All we must do is uncover them, and you'll do this step by step by taking the actions in each chapter.

When I made the leap into Accidental Entrepreneurship— which, by the way, looked like me sitting at my kitchen table with my laptop and having more questions than I had answers—one of the first things I did was start reading and listening to other entrepreneurs.

This was great as I started to learn from incredible people who I now call mentors that don't know my name (yet!), but a lot of noise arose that I didn't resonate with at all. Knowing the difference between what's helpful and what's noise is going to vary person by person but the filter is the same:

After receiving the information, ask yourself, "Why do I believe I need to take this action?"

If it's because you're genuinely excited or curious about how it can help you or your business, then it's helpful information. This doesn't mean it will be helpful forever, but in this season of business, consuming it is helpful.

If you notice that you feel like you "should" be doing something simply because someone else said to, but it doesn't quite sit well with you, then it's likely noise. This doesn't mean the information is bad; it simply means it's not helpful for you in this moment.

The one caveat to this is to make sure you run it through the "is this a law or recommended for legal reasons" filter. There are things that may feel like a "should" task but that are actually something you need to do to protect your business. Some of these include:

- registering your business so you can make money legally

- setting up a business bank account to ensure your business and personal finances are separate

- purchasing business insurance so you and your business are protected in specific situations

This book doesn't go into legal or accounting details, so I highly recommend consulting with attorneys, accountants, and insurance agents. Referrals from other entrepreneurs are a great place to start.

WHY LISTEN TO WHAT I SAY

I want to make it clear from the beginning; I'm not perfect at anything I will share, nor do I believe perfect is possible. My motto is "done is better than perfect" when it comes to taking action in my business, and because of this I mess up a lot. But I learn fast and do my very best to share my lessons with others.

The way that I share these lessons as a coach is through my podcast *The Unapologetic Entrepreneur* and virtual programs. During my career as an entrepreneur, I've hosted group coaching programs and created courses and a membership. While the offerings have and will likely continue to change, the focus remains consistent. My passion is helping entrepreneurs make progress toward building the business of their dreams.

While my expertise, education, and corporate experience is in marketing, I've also helped my clients in other areas. Inside all my programs there is a focus on identifying a goal and then taking intentional and consistent action toward that goal, whether it be creating a website or navigating the fear of selling an offering.

Progress is the focus because that's the only thing that's between you and what you desire. I know this is easier said than done as action to create progress takes courage, but just as I've taken small steps, I'll guide you in taking those steps, so you can make progress toward your own success.

I started my company in 2017 after being laid off from a corporate job; talk about an accident! I had no idea what I was doing, but I figured it out one google search, book, and podcast at a time. I didn't go to business school, but I didn't let that stop me; I was, and still am, determined to learn.

While I do have a background that I'm very proud of, that's not what gets me through all the tough stuff of being an entrepreneur. Sure, it helps my confidence when I remember that I finished my master's graduate thesis even though it was *soooo* hard. But equally so, I'm proud of the time in my business when I hosted an online training that 905 people signed up for. Or the fact that my business is 100 percent debt free, and I pay myself every month. And I'm proud of the hundreds of "thank you Amanda" emails and messages I receive because I followed this passion. I'll never get enough of those.

These are things that also help uncover my confidence and help me take the next step, just like you're ready to do now. Yes, it's scary when you have no clue what's coming next, but look back at your past accomplishments and remember you've done hard things, so you can do this too.

Everything in this book is aimed to help you navigate this bumpy road of entrepreneurship, and I can't wait to dig in. But before we do, don't miss this moment my friend.

Look up. Take it in. Be a tourist in this city of entrepreneurship. I can't wait to see your pictures!

PART 1

WHY YOU WANT TO BE AN ENTREPRENEUR

By knowing this, you set a strong foundation for long-term success.

CHAPTER 1

YOUR Y.O.U. PROMISE

———

Many frameworks delineate how to create a business, and they all center around the business needs such as sales, customers, and systems. While these are all important, the key component to a successful business for the Accidental Entrepreneur is *you*.

The person who's starting this company, no matter how big it becomes.

The person who's building it from the ground up.

The person who's brave enough to say, "I want to build a business that feels right for me."

You've picked up this book because you've identified the fire inside you to start or grow your business. It might just be a tiny ember now, or maybe it's a full-fledged fire; regardless, it's time to fan that fire and make things happen. But as you take action, you'll likely have questions like this running through your mind:

Who am I to try this?

Is now the best time to take this risk?

I had the same thoughts as I entered my first networking event after getting laid off from a corporate job. I signed up for the event on my third day of being laid off, and I was excited to attend until I parked my car outside. Then it hit me...

What am I going to say when someone asks me what I do or where I work?

The ache in my stomach at that moment was enough to have me drive home and hide in bed, but I'm proud to say I didn't do that. I figured it would only last an hour, and free breakfast sounded like the right price for someone who was recently laid off.

I wrote my name on the name tag, left the company line blank, and then it happened: The first person asked me what I did for work. (Imagine a long pause and the sweat starting.) I shook her hand and said, "I'm Amanda, and I'm in between careers right now and trying to figure that out."

You know what happened next? She smiled and said something like this: "That's awesome. A new slate, good for you. I hope whatever doors you want to open will open for you."

I wish I could hug that woman today because of the impact she had on my life, and she likely doesn't know it. Had she reacted in a negative or even neutral way, I may have been shier about admitting to someone else during the event that I was thinking about starting a consulting business. That was how my ember started—one conversation where

I was brave enough to say, "I'm thinking of starting a consulting business."

That ember became a little bigger as I continued to share this idea with others who were supportive, but I was still doubting myself as an entrepreneur. Maybe this is where you are and thoughts about waiting until you have more money saved up or you get that next degree or training are constantly running through your mind.

Or maybe you've started your business and you made it over that initial roadblock of uncovering your confidence to start, but now you're feeling stuck. This is something that happened to me four years into business after I had achieved many revenue-related milestones I had set for myself. Even after hitting my goals, I still felt scattered which led to me doubting my abilities. Maybe you doubt if you can continue because it feels like such an uphill battle, or you feel scattered with everything in your business.

These are all legit questions, but I want to counter them with a few others:

Why not you?

Why not now?

Why not on your terms?

You have everything you need to achieve success based on your definition. You have a unique perspective on life that will benefit others, and they are waiting to hear from you.

And there will never be a time that feels completely "right" whether you're looking to start or looking to scale.

Good news awaits, though. You can get through the muck and gain the momentum you're looking for through what I call your Y.O.U. Promise.

YOUR Y.O.U. PROMISE

By tapping into Y.O.U. Promise, you're able to set a strong foundation for your business that will allow you to start and scale no matter what comes your way. This promise is not one created for a specific business type but rather a type of person: the Accidental Entrepreneur who wants to create a business that integrates into their life rather than taking over it.

Creating your Y.O.U. Promise is as simple as answering a few questions. Just like your GPS can redirect you when there's a detour, this is what your Y.O.U. Promise will do for you. It will help guide you back to steady ground to create a sense of security, so you can gain the momentum you're searching for at any stage of business. This becomes your compass.

Your Y.O.U. Promise is made up of three sections:

Y—why *you* want to be an entrepreneur

O—opportunity to define your values and success

U—unapologetically use what works for you

Y—Why You Want to Be an Entrepreneur

It starts with your deep-down-honest "why" for being an Accidental Entrepreneur, and this will set your foundation for your success.

We will address this in Part 1 of the book.

O—Opportunity to Define Your Values & Success

Adding your core values and defining success on your terms builds on the strong foundation, so you have clarity on your path forward.

We will address this in Part 2 of the book.

U—Unapologetically Use What Works for You

Once you have your destination set, you can determine the methods and tools that will help you achieve success on your terms. These include setting boundaries, identifying your support system, tapping into your strengths, understanding your finances, and setting goals.

We will address this in Part 3 of the book.

Once you have declared your Y.O.U. Promise, it becomes your guide to success. As you're faced with decisions in your business, when you're feeling scattered, when nothing seems to be working, these are times when you come back to your Y.O.U. Promise.

Your Y.O.U. Promise will serve you no matter what twists and turns come your way as an entrepreneur. You may shut one business down and start another, and your Y.O.U. Promise will guide you. You may need to pivot your current business, and your Y.O.U. Promise will guide you.

This is a promise you're making to yourself to create a business that integrates into your life instead of taking it over. By making a few declarations, you will have a strong foundation to make this a reality. Now that you know the concept, it's time to dig into details of declaring your Y.O.U. Promise.

KEY TAKEAWAYS:

- Embracing your Y.O.U. Promise will be your guide to achieving your definition of success.

- Understanding your deep-down-honest why is the key to a strong business foundation.

- As an Accidental Entrepreneur, you can define your core values and what success means for you.

- Throughout your journey, finding the methods and systems that work for you will continue your path to success.

To help you define your Y.O.U. Promise, I've created a workbook that you can access for free at amandamckinney.com/more.

CHAPTER 2

YOUR DEEP-DOWN-HONEST WHY

———

I've become known for something by my clients, and it's that I ask "why" whenever we're talking about goals. I want the word "goal" to be followed by "why" every time it's mentioned.

Goal, *why*.

Goal, *why*.

Goal, *why*.

The reason I sound like a broken record is because of how much it matters, but this doesn't just apply to goals.

It matters on a much deeper level because it impacts your entrepreneurship success overall, and that's why it's the first piece of your Y.O.U. Promise. If you aren't clear on why you want to be an entrepreneur, your chances of success are low, but if you're clear on your why, you have a much higher probability of succeeding on your terms.

This is easier to see when you take a step back from your overall business and look at goals:

Think back to the last time you achieved a goal you set.

Now, ask yourself *why* you wanted to achieve that goal.

Think back to the last time you didn't achieve a goal you set.

Now ask yourself *why* you wanted to achieve that goal.

Chances are, when you didn't achieve your goal, your why wasn't stronger than the pushback you experienced from your current habits or circumstances. This is the reason that understanding your why is critical when it comes to your Accidental Entrepreneurship journey.

Your why is the reason you want to pursue entrepreneurship.

Your why is the real, deep-down-honest answer. Not the one that you would likely tell someone else right away. The one that's so deep down in your heart that you might even have to dig to find it. I'm here to help you discover that, so you can have the strongest foundation possible.

WHY YOUR WHY MATTERS
If you know your why, you'll figure out the "how."

Please read that again, slowly, so it really sinks in because this is the reason it matters. Just a few sentences ago I asked you to reflect on a time when you achieved a goal and why you wanted to achieve that goal. Whether it was learning to speak Spanish (so you could travel and feel safe), tracking your sleep (so you could have more energy during the day), or something completely different, what I want you to recognize is that you knew your why and figured out the how.

Now, think back to the journey to achieving that goal, and ask yourself if you had to change the how at least once? Twice? More times than you can remember?

Most of the time, we don't get the how right on the first try, and this is when there's a fork in the road. You either:

1. Try a different method and see if it works

2. Stop trying

This is where you can tell if your why is stronger than the resistance you're encountering and the reason your why matters more than your passion.

For example, let's say you're a baker and have a strong passion for creating sweet treats. You decide to open a bakery and experience a great start at your grand opening. After two years, you hit tough times, and customers are few and far between, but the rent payment is consistent.

This is the fork-in-the-road moment. You can either try different approaches to increase business, or you can continue doing the same thing until you're forced to cancel your building lease. Your actions in this moment are what reveal if your why is stronger than the resistance of hard times.

Or maybe you're a consultant that has a passion for helping people see results in their marketing, but your true why for starting your business is so that you can be in control of your schedule, what you work on, and who you work with. After achieving the initial goals, things start to trend downward. Instead of continuing down the same path, you consider other options, so you can continue to be an entrepreneur even if it looks different.

By the way, that second one is my example. While I'd love to tell you I was clear on my why from the beginning, that would be a lie, but it became clear to me at the first fork-in-the-road moment. That moment was when my business revenue started trending downward for the first time.

Staring at the spreadsheet, I had a choice to make: Either try something different, or continue doing the same thing and expecting a different result. While the feelings of doubt and concern were immediate, the actions I took soon after that are what indicated my why was stronger than the resistance I was facing.

I began brainstorming other ideas I could try to gain clients. I learned from online searches and taking one small step at a time, even though I didn't know what would work. The key was that I was willing to try different approaches because my why of wanting control of my schedule was strong.

Your why is truly revealed to you during tough times, whether or not you identified it beforehand. This is a wonderful silver lining to the tough times because they do show up, and finding the silver lining when they do is important.

To be clear, you can absolutely make money in your business without truly understanding the reason you're starting your business, but at some point you will find yourself in a tough time when you meet that fork in the road. Your actions will indicate if your why is strong enough, and since you're reading this and will identify your why, you'll have a much stronger foundation to navigate the detours along the way.

HOW TO UNCOVER YOUR WHY

While there is no wrong answer to the question "why do you want to start your own business" or "why did you start your own business," the key is that you're honest with yourself, and the answer is strong enough to get you through the times of uncertainty and self-doubt.

For this exercise of figuring out your deep-down-honest why, we need to start by knowing the difference between your passion and your why.

YOUR PASSION IS ABOUT *OTHER PEOPLE.*

When most people describe their business, they are talking about their passion, and you'll do this too. It often sounds like this:

Your Passion = helping (insert who you help) with (insert what you help them with)

(E.g., helping stressed out women make time for themselves without the guilt)

Your passion is critical to your business because *"people don't buy what you do; they buy why you do it"* (Sinek 2009).

This is often missed by many new entrepreneurs because we are fixated on the how. Most of us (raising my hand) love to start with the how. This often looks something like this:

- You have an idea.

- You immediately figure out how to create the solution.

- You try and sell the solution and feel the pressure of competition.

While competitors will always offer similar solutions as you, the feeling of competition doesn't have to be present. When you feel this pressure creeping in, you're likely focused on the how more than your passion for solving this particular problem. But don't get down on yourself; this is natural and part of the process.

Identifying how to do something is what we're taught and trained to do. You're presented with a math problem, and you have to figure out how to solve it. You see a sink full of dishes and an almost full dishwasher, and you figure out how to fit them all in there like it's a Tetris game you want to win.

We launch into how to solve something before asking "why do I want to solve this?" And while we don't need to pause before we load the dishwasher, taking time to truly identify your why behind starting a business is critical if you want to be in this for the long haul.

This passion of yours will help you most days and is certainly a driving force in your business, but your passion will not help you on days when you're crying on the bathroom floor because everything, and I mean everything, feels like it's crumbling.

Sales are down.

You have multiple tech issues.

Family members are upset.

You're sick.

When you run into this situation, or something similar, your passion for helping someone with something will not help you keep going, but your deep-down-honest why will help you pull through.

YOUR WHY IS ABOUT *YOU*.
This is something you won't hear very often from others, and it's not likely that you'll share this with others either. This is more internal, and it looks like this:

Your why = I'm an entrepreneur so that I can (insert your why).

(E.g., I'm an entrepreneur so that I can be in control of my schedule, what I work on, and who I work with.)

See the difference between the two things? Your passion is critical to your success as an Accidental Entrepreneur as it will guide what your business looks like and helps you fulfill your why, but your why is the key component to longevity in entrepreneurship.

Another way to think about this is that your passion can (and likely will) change many times in your entrepreneurship journey, but your why will likely stay the same. You may start seven businesses in your lifetime, all with different passions and equally as fulfilling for you, but the reason behind continuing to be an entrepreneur will be the same.

Going with a generic answer to the question "why do I want to be/continue being an entrepreneur?" is likely tempting, but your deep-down-honest answer will help you the most. I encourage you to spend time with this question so that you can set your business on the strongest foundation possible, even if you're discovering this answer years into business.

On that note, please remember that where you are in your Accidental Entrepreneurship journey is exactly where you're supposed to be today. Just like people restore older homes and place new supports in the foundation to make it stronger, you can do the same with your existing business.

It's time to declare your first piece of your Y.O.U. Promise:

Y—why you want to be an entrepreneur

O—opportunity to define your values and success

U—unapologetically use what works for you

As you explore your why, be sure to give yourself space and grace for this exercise. Being honest and digging deep to know this answer can often be difficult and take time.

KEY TAKEAWAYS:

- The first declaration in your Y.O.U. Promise is your why.

- Your passion is about others and will help guide what your business looks like.

- Your why is about you and will help you through the tough times in entrepreneurship.

RECOMMENDED ACTIONS:

1. Give yourself permission to be honest about your why, and remember that you don't have to share this with anyone else.

2. Ask yourself why you want to be an entrepreneur. (Optional: Think back to a fork-in-the-road moment if you've had one, and reflect what actions you took and why you took them. What kept you going?)

3. Continue to ask why until you get to the deep-down-honest answer that's about you, not your customers.

4. Say your why out loud. Write it down, so you can see it. The key is to know your why, so it's accessible when you hit a hard time. If you like to keep things visual, you can make it your computer background image, or have a sticky note on your bathroom mirror.

PART 2

OPPORTUNITY TO DEFINE YOUR VALUES & SUCCESS

What you will chase in your Accidental Entrepreneurship journey is critical to define so that you stay focused.

CHAPTER 3

CLAIM TRUE-TO-YOU VALUES

You might be curious how personal and business values connect or if they do at all.

I believe they connect 100 percent as you, the Accidental Entrepreneur starting this business, are leading the business. Whether you intend to hire others or not, you are the leader so your personal values will overlap into business, even though they will be phrased differently.

For example, one of my personal values is appreciation. In all the years of living my life, I've never seen "appreciation" on a list of values, but through an exercise I'll share with you in this chapter as the next part of your Y.O.U Promise, this word was all the way at the top for me.

I naturally show appreciation when something kind is done for me, and I ensure the person knows how grateful I am. Likewise, if I don't feel appreciated, it really bothers me. While I don't do things for recognition, I do value being appreciated.

Once I recognized this, I thought about how this has impacted my business, and it very quickly became clear. One example is that I prioritize sending personal messages even when it doesn't make sense from a time perspective. As the business owner, I know that showing appreciation to those who work for/with me as well as my clients is critical to me, and therefore it will impact how my team and I work.

Here's how my value of appreciation is defined in my business:

You Are Appreciated:

We make our appreciation known to those we work with. We believe that when people know they are valued, they can move forward and create a bigger ripple effect in this world in a positive way.

Did you notice that this value definition feels more personal than the typical "teamwork" posters you'd see on a corporate office wall to describe a company value? This is intentional, and you can do this too.

My friend Danait Berhe, who's also a brand and messaging strategist, told me this: Let your personality shine through when you share your values.

This was helpful to hear, and I hope you take her advice too because a true-to-you-value is one that sounds and feels like you.

Another example of true-to-you-values is from someone who has influenced my business in many ways that I'll share throughout this book, and his name is Mike Michalowicz. Mike is an author of many best-selling books and is on a mission to eradicate entrepreneurial poverty. I just love that!

He's open about entrepreneurship and what has helped (and hurt) him as an entrepreneur. But one of my favorite stories is about a key value of his. This value is... no dicks allowed. Seriously, those words exactly helped move his business forward while staying true to himself:

> When I wanted money to fund my book, I wrote a vision statement for investors, and on it, I placed a yellow sticky note with the statement that read "No Dicks Allowed." I wanted my business to be known for and characterized by genuineness and authenticity. No one involved in my business was permitted to be a "dick"—no vendors, clients—no one. My accountant, when he read the note, said, "Mike, you can't say that!" I replied, "But that's who I am." The next day, I received a Fedex package from one investor with a check for $100,000. The investor said, "I'm not a dick, and I'm in" (Caprino 2013).

This is what I mean by true-to-you values. You don't have to put yourself into a box that you don't fit in; you can create the box. Don't start with a list of words that someone else wrote down, start your own list by looking inward to find what truly matters to you.

Whether you follow Mike and say "no dicks allowed" or choose a word like "appreciation" or something in between, the only thing that matters is that it's true to you.

HOW VALUES HELP YOUR BUSINESS

At some point, most new Accidental Entrepreneurs ask (or at least think) the question, "Who am I to try and do this? There are other people doing this, why should I try?"

This comes into play as we start our business and throughout our journey as things evolve. We aren't immune to this thought no matter how much education or experience we have. Self-doubt can creep in quickly, and if we don't catch it, it can derail our progress.

My tool to counteract these questions when I'm coaching someone is to remind them that even though others are doing something similar, no one can replicate what they can provide. We are all unique human beings that have unique experiences that influence what we offer in our business, and our values are one component of this.

Your values help differentiate you from your competitors.

Remember, people buy why we offer something, not only what we are offering. You can see this in your own behavior as you made the choice to purchase this book. You likely read the title, the description, and maybe some quotes from others. You were reading to identify if you resonated with me and how I teach specifically.

Thousands of books on entrepreneurship exist, but you identified this as one you wanted to invest your financial resources in, and for that I'm grateful. Part of the reason you purchased this book is because it was written by me, not someone else.

People will do the same for you in your business. When we share our authentic selves as the Accidental Entrepreneur behind the offering, we can truly connect with the person considering our offering.

"When leaders act and make decisions according to the company's workplace values, they outperform their counterparts by 27 percent" (Transcend 2022).

How would it feel to have an immediate jump of 27 percent in performance in your business?

Answer = A—MA—ZING!

This stat stunned me at first, but once I really thought through it, it made sense. Because when we are aligned with our values, we operate in a more effective and efficient way. We're less likely to get caught up in the "should trap" and go along with whatever the new fad is in the business world.

Business values help you to:

- make business decisions that are in alignment with you and your dreams

- have structure that leads to more career satisfaction

Your values also have a heavy influence on hiring employees but even if you're not planning that yet, they are still important. All the work you do in this area of your business while you're a solo entrepreneur will help you as you expand your team, hire contractors, or make decisions about systems and software you will use.

For example, if a core value of yours is accessibility and as you're evaluating different software options you realize that one doesn't allow for transcription of audio, but another does, that would help you make a decision.

Your values will also help you stay motivated as you establish and build your business: "Learning science experts say that a primary driver of unmotivated employee behavior is a mismatch in values" (Transcend 2022). But this isn't just for employees; it matters for the leader too.

If you feel misaligned with your business, you will be unmotivated.

Think back to a time where you were pumped about something and then lost interest. Maybe it was a job, maybe it was a hobby, regardless, you had an interest and lost it. Can you remember what caused that loss of interest?

For me, this was my Facebook group. I started my Facebook group in 2018, and it grew to a few thousand people. For a while it served an amazing purpose. It helped me connect with new people, share my message as I was starting out, and gave me a place to answer questions for free. All great things as you're first starting out as an entrepreneur, but things evolve in business.

After a few years of running the Facebook group, I felt the urge to close it down as it wasn't feeling in alignment with my value of authenticity. I found myself encouraging others to let go of things that they didn't want to do or that didn't feel right to them, all the while I was holding on to this Facebook Group because I thought I "should." Or even more "it might be helpful one day." It's like the shirt in your closet that you "might wear again one day" but instead it takes up space for five years, and you eventually give it away.

I paused the Facebook Group for three months to see how it felt and to see if anything changed in my business or in my heart. After three months, I looked back at the data and my emotions and realized that it was time to let the group go. This decision could have gone either way, but once I realized the lack of motivation for this particular action was a misalignment with my values, it was time to let it go.

Whether you're running into this feeling today or you hit it a year from now, remember this quick test and that you can pause something most of the time before completely cutting it out if that feels better for you. And you can always start something again if it needs to come back.

DEFINING YOUR VALUES

It's time to go back to your Y.O.U. Promise, and work through the second part which defines what you will be working toward in your business. You know *why* you're ready to go down this path, so now it's time to define *what* your destination is.

Y—why you want to be an entrepreneur

O—opportunity to define your values and success

U—unapologetically use what works for you

As an Accidental Entrepreneur who is likely working solo, you might be thinking, "I don't need to do this yet." And you know what? Getting started without having this set in stone or even written in sand is okay.

Just like you can make money before understanding your deep-down-honest why behind being an entrepreneur, you can absolutely make money without defining your values. However, taking time to work through this exercise will continue to build on the strong foundation for your business and give you a competitive advantage from the beginning.

When it comes to going through this process, there are options:

1. DIY this exercise knowing you can always refine it later.

2. Work with a strategist/coach to help you.

DIYING THE VALUES EXERCISE

The exercise outlined below is what worked for me, but there are many free or paid options online that you can investigate as well.

These reflections are from an exercise from the Co-Active Training Institute, and it includes a values clarification exercise (Co-Active Training Institute, n.d.):

1. A peak moment in time—looking for moments that were particularly rewarding for you

2. Suppressed values—use the opposite and look for time when you were angry, frustrated, or upset

3. Must-haves—asking yourself what you need in your life in order to be fulfilled (other than the necessities)

Remember the example about my value of appreciation? I uncovered that value when I explored suppressed values. Finding the things that aren't going well or that we wish were happening is often easier. While I don't suggest that you fixate on this for too long, I suggest this as the best place to start as you'll get clear information, quickly.

Grab your pencil and use the workbook that accompanies this book for this exercise. You can download the workbook at amandamckinney.com/more

STEP 1:

Ask yourself, "When have I recently felt upset or frustrated with something?" and see what comes up for you. This could be related to business or your personal life because, remember, they are connected.

I suggest timing this exercise and only giving yourself ten minutes to think of an example and write down any thoughts related to that example. Write down anything that comes to mind, and don't worry about it being in complete sentences or identifying any specific value at this point.

An example of this could look like:

- She didn't say thank you.
- I don't know if what I did actually helped.
- Unsure.
- Scattered, like I'm throwing spaghetti at the wall.

STEP 2:
Now it's time to shift gears and ask yourself, "When have I recently felt joy, happiness, or abundance?" and capture what comes up for you. Again, this can be business or personal, and you don't have to worry about identifying a word during this ten-minute exercise.

An example of this could look like:

- I lost track of time, and it felt great.
- Crossed items off the to-do list with time to spare.
- Time alone—that felt great.

STEP 3:
Since those were reflecting on specific instances, you want to make sure to capture your must-haves in life too. These are the things you already know need to be on the list in order to have a fulfilling life and business. Take just five minutes to reflect on anything in this category, although you might not need a full five minutes.

An example of this could look like:

- Peace and calm—striving for this in my daily life is important to me.
- Aesthetics—surrounding myself with things I find beautiful helps creativity.
- Organization—when things feel scattered (physically in my space or emotionally) being productive is hard.

STEP 4:
It's time to pull it all together. First, make note of any themes you notice emerging, but if they don't jump out at you, that's also okay. If you didn't immediately notice any particular themes/words, read your bullet points out loud and think about the specific examples and if they have any connection.

For example, when I did this exercise, I noted a few things in different categories that came together to form the value of independence. These things were:

- Solo trip where I did whatever I felt like doing.
- Nothing is on my schedule for an entire day; I can do whatever is important.
- Sharing information that allows people to take it and use what works for them.

This led to my value of independence that I define as:

Choose What's Best for You:

We share resources in a way that allows you to make decisions that feel right to you. We believe there isn't a one-size-fits-all strategy for entrepreneurs but that you can learn from the paths of others.

Give yourself time to identify your values through this exercise, and also give yourself grace as you explore. Your goal is to identify three to five words or phrases that will serve as your values.

STEP 5:
Check in with how you're living your values every quarter. I will elaborate on this more in the Goals chapter, but I suggest doing business check-ins every ninety days. These check-ins are great times to assess your values to ensure that you're staying aligned with them. Here are some quick check-ins you can do with your values:

- Do you actually remember them? Ideally, you want to know these so well that it's easy for you to talk about them if someone asks you about them.
- Are you living them? If you took an inventory of your actions, can you see your values reflected?
- Does anything need to change? We and our businesses will evolve, and while our values are less likely to evolve as much, things change sometimes. If needed, change your list of values, so you can continue to live your values.

WORKING WITH A COACH/STRATEGIST

If you have the budget to work with a coach on this process, it's a great option as having someone else walk you through this exercise can often be extremely helpful. However, you also might be more reserved with your thoughts, so be sure that you find someone you trust and can be open with.

As you evaluate people to help you in this process, here are some questions to consider:

- What is your budget for this project?
- Is the coach specialized in defining values? (This isn't a necessity, but it's important to note.)
- Do you believe you can be open with this person as you define values that are personal to you?

One way to gauge your comfort level is to consume free or paid content from the coach. Most entrepreneurship coaches have online content you can consume which gives you a good sense of if you resonate with how they coach. I suggest taking some actions that they suggest to see how those actions work for you and if you feel aligned with that particular person.

Another way to get to know the coach is if they have a free or paid consultation call. Not everyone offers these, but some coaches offer a short, one-time call where you can ask questions to get a feel if you would work well with them and vice versa. I suggest booking a consultation call with them before committing to working through values.

Regardless of the method you choose to define your values, these will guide not only your business success but also your happiness within your business. As you're on the path to chasing your definition of success unapologetically, this is a key part of the process. Be sure to take the time to define your values so that you can truly create a strong foundation for your business.

KEY TAKEAWAYS:

- Defining your values is part of the O in your Y.O.U. Promise.

- Personal and business values are connected.

- Your business values impact your success.

- You can hire someone or DIY defining your business values.

RECOMMENDED ACTIONS:

1. Identify if you will hire a coach or DIY your values exercise.

2. If you choose to hire a coach, take the steps to find the best coach for you.

3. If you choose to DIY the exercise, take the steps outlined in this exercise.

4. Optional: Put your values on the About page of your business website.

CHAPTER 4

DEFINE SUCCESS ON YOUR TERMS

———

How do you define success?

Chances are you've never defined this for yourself. You've likely declared goals, but goals are milestones we set to achieve success.

Wait? What?

Let's say that again: Goals are milestones we set to achieve success.

If that was just a lightbulb moment for you, I am right there with you. A few years ago, I was confronted with the reality that I wasn't going to hit my goal of making six figures in my business, and it was very frustrating. As I navigated this truth, I did what I always do and looked for the lesson in the "failure."

This looks like me writing and reflecting on what happened during that particular experience and talking it through with a coach and some of my "biz besties" (more on them later). As I reflected both in writing and talking, I had the aha moment.

One of my biz besties asked, "What is success for you?" and I answered by sharing the goal I was working toward. She asked again and that's when I realized that success and goals are different, but I was treating them as if they were the same.

It was clear that I needed to define success for myself, and so the journey began. It took a while for me to have a definition that I was comfortable saying was done, but I finally got there.

Currently, success to me means being present in my life and content with what I have, while also challenging myself in new ways.

This definition spans into all areas of my life including my business, and I landed on this definition after many, many months of really digging into this. I'll walk you through my exercise at the end of this chapter so you can start your journey of defining success for yourself as the next piece of your Y.O.U. Promise.

INSPIRATION FROM OTHERS

While developing your definition of success doesn't have a formula, getting inspired from others is often helpful. As I was on the journey of defining what success meant for me, which included me writing this book, I found many examples, and some of the most memorable and inspiring definitions I came across were defined by people with disabilities:

- To me, having a successful life is being able to do things independently for myself and not always have someone there to do things for me. It's achieving my goals on my own terms and at my own pace. (high school student with a mobility impairment)

- Success is a relative term. If you achieve what you want to and are happy, then I think that is success. It could be applied to life in general or to individual tasks in life. (college student with a mobility impairment)

- My definition of success is achieving personal goals, whatever they may be. Some goals are considered small by some people and enormous by others. What matters is that they are personal; each individual has his/her own formula for personal success. (college student who is deaf)

- I remember what my high school voice teacher told the class as we prepared for our senior solo. She said, "Success comes in *cans*, and failure comes in *can'ts*." (speech language pathologist who is blind)

- Succeeding is accomplishing my dreams. However slowly I am moving toward that, to some degree, I am succeeding. (high school student who is blind)

- Even though you might not have obtained that set goal, you are successful if you tried your best. (college student with a brain injury)

- To me, success is being able to do whatever it takes to lead a productive life. (young person who is blind)

- Success? That's an easy one. *Be happy.* (high school student with a learning disability)

(DOIT 2022).

I just loved the honesty and simplicity that many of these definitions of success contain, and they inspired me to think outside the business box that I was in when I first started to define success.

Specifically, as Accidental Entrepreneurs we tend to think about money as the barometer to success because we're focused on the revenue in business. While this metric in your business is important, it's not the only contributor to success, and this seems easier to understand once your financial needs are met.

A business mentor of mine, Kate Ahl, the founder of Simple Pin Media, said it this way:

> In year one and two, success was all financial. "Am I getting a paycheck?"

> Then in years three to five, success was "Am I making a difference?"

> Then in years six and beyond, success has been "What will the legacy be?"

One of my biz besties, Megan Spears, a yoga teacher and physical therapy student, said it like this:

> If you asked me this several years ago, I would have said more about money, but because I'm comfortable with where I am financially, I am now concerned with my time.

Another business mentor of mine, Mike Basch, a managing partner at Atento Capital, said this:

> I was unapologetically motivated to be in better financial circumstances than my parents were. That worked until I was thirty, and I woke up on my birthday really feeling empty inside. There wasn't a strong sense of purpose. So, I took a sabbatical from my business to reflect on what I wanted to do. And now what gets me going is that I have a passion for unlocking human potential.

Did you catch the theme? Throughout my journey to define success as an Accidental Entrepreneur myself, I found two themes that emerged in the interviews, research, and my own reflection:

1. Our definitions of success evolve with the seasons of our lives.

2. Our definitions usually start with a financial focus, but they often change to time/flexibility/quality of life.

As you begin the journey of defining success for yourself, please remember these two trends. It's likely that you'll start this process and feel uncomfortable setting a definition because it can feel like it's written in stone, but it's more like written in sand (or on a whiteboard if that's more your thing).

You have the freedom to adjust your definition as your seasons of life change, but this doesn't mean the target is always moving. Rather, think about your definition of success more like a destination you're looking forward to visiting. In one season of your life, the beach may be calling your name, but in another season, the mountains are.

Success is the destination you're looking to make it to, but changing the destination is okay.

YOUR "SO THAT" SENTENCE

As I continued my journey to define success, I interviewed others on the topic and noticed a distinct pattern in how people shared their definitions. When I asked this question, it was usually met with a long pause before an answer came. This in itself was fascinating to me because it demonstrated that not many people define success for themselves.

Through these interviews, I realized I wasn't alone in lumping goals and success together; we all tend to do this. But after the long pause I heard things like:

- "Being able to be with friends and family. Being able to drop things when I need to and take care of someone in my family when I need to. To have a quiet routine **where I** feel like I have more space in my calendar. That's what success feels like to me."

- "Am I waking up every day, feeling like I have a sense of purpose, and I'm working toward the impact I want to make in the world? Am I **moving closer** to the person that I ultimately want to become?"

- "I make decisions that **allow me** to have the financial success that I want **while also** maintaining my sanity and my time freedom."

- "When I first began my business at twenty-five, success looked like freedom of location. I could live on my own terms wherever I wanted to live. And now in this season of my life, success looks like freedom but in terms of flexibility **so that** I can stop work at noon and spend time with my daughter until she goes to sleep."

I kept noticing the bolded words, and it hit me… we all have a "so that" part of our definition. We want something "so that" we can get something else. It all comes back to the *why* behind what we're striving for.

As you begin to identify what success means for you, watch for the "so that" part of your definition. You may use different words, but you'll see it come through. For example:

- *Success means bringing home $50,000 every year because **when I do that,** I have an extra $500 per month to surprise a few people with a gift that month.*

- *Success means contributing $2,000 a month to my family budget, **so I'm** helping pay the bills, but I also don't work in the evenings **so that** I get to make dinner at night for the family.*

Whatever follows the "so that" part of your sentence is what it really boils down to for you. The number is the defined amount, but it's *why* you want to make that specific amount that really matters.

Do you see how everything comes back to why? This is the reason your why is so important and the reason it's the first part of your Y.O.U. Promise. When we understand why we want to chase something or see something in our bank account, we can then have a better understanding of who we want to be and how we want to show up in our lives. This is what I want for you.

YOU ARE WORTHY OF DEFINING SUCCESS FOR YOURSELF

Before we dive into the nitty-gritty of the exercise for defining success for yourself, there's one thing we must talk about first:

You deserve whatever definition of success you set for yourself.

I bring this up because of the number of times I've been coaching or speaking on this topic and received resistance to this exercise. I remember one time so well it still makes me tear up if I stop and think about it. I was speaking and mentioned defining success, and a lady came up to me afterward and said something close to, "I'm uncomfortable defining success because I don't feel worthy to actually achieve it."

I immediately asked if I could hug her because I was so touched by her bravery to say that out loud to someone she barely knew. After our embrace, I told her exactly what I just mentioned to you.

You are worthy of whatever definition of success you set for yourself. And I'll back this up even more with the question, "Why not you?"

You encourage others as they chase success for themselves. *Why not you?*

You like social media posts of others sharing their success stories. *Why not you?*

You're the first one to send a congrats card to your friend. *Why not you?*

While many factors could contribute to feeling this way, when it comes to entrepreneurship, my guess is imposter syndrome. Imposter syndrome is *"someone who feels they aren't as capable as others think and fears they'll be exposed as a fraud"* (Benisek 2022).

You're convinced that others are doing it better or that you're not qualified enough to start the business that's on your mind and heart. And before you get down on yourself for thinking like this, I want to remind you that you aren't alone in this. All entrepreneurs (and really, all humans) are subject to imposter syndrome, and many very prominent and successful people have spoken out about this, so you're certainly not alone if you fall prey to this.

Maya Angelou said, "I have written eleven books, but each time I think, 'Uh oh, they're going to find out now. I've run a game on everybody, and they're going to find me out'" (Talbot 2021).

Emma Watson said, "When I receive recognition for my acting, I feel incredibly uncomfortable. I tend to turn in on myself. I feel like an imposter" (Talbot 2021).

Tom Hanks said, "No matter what we've done, there comes a point when you think; How did I get here? When are they going to discover that I am, in fact, a fraud and take everything away from me?" (Talbot 2021).

While I know it's easier said than done, it's time to move through imposter syndrome, so you can truly define success for yourself, and then go get it!

If you're feeling doubtful currently, I encourage you to think about trying to define success as if you were walking your friend through this exercise. Imagine that you're encouraging someone to get clear on this so they can create the business and life of their dreams, but then do this for yourself.

If you need a pep talk, stop reading and listen to episode #39 on my podcast, *The Unapologetic Entrepreneur.*

HOW TO DEFINE SUCCESS FOR YOURSELF

While you can go about defining success for yourself in many ways, this exercise helped me ultimately get to a definition. The idea is that you start with what you've declared already in your Y.O.U. Promise, and expand on that to find your definition of success.

Y—why you want to be an entrepreneur

O—opportunity to define your values and success on your terms

U—unapologetically use what works for you

As you go into this exercise, think of success as the destination you're trying to get to but not in the sense that it will always be far away. Your definition of success can be the destination you strive to arrive at daily. You can use this exercise to define success for your business only, or you can look at all aspects of your life.

Step 1:

Start by reviewing your Y.O.U. Promise that includes your why and core values. From those notes, ask yourself, "Do I want to carry over any words or phrases into my success definition?" If so, write those down at the top of a piece of paper.

Step 2:

Ask yourself, "When did I last feel successful?" Write down that experience and why it felt successful to you. Pay close attention to why it felt successful, not only the result you achieved. This is the "so that" part of your experience, and it will reveal the most to you.

Step 3:

Based on your values and an example of success in your life, write a draft of your definition of success. Don't worry, it's just a draft at this point. Write it down in a place where you can see it every day because you will revisit this daily for a month. Your definition can include your "so that" sentence, but it's not required. There isn't a one-size-fits-all formula for this, but since it's often easiest to start from somewhere, here is a good starting place:

Success to me means (insert your words or phrases) so that I (insert what this will allow you to do/be).

Step 4:

Review your draft by reading or writing it daily for at least a month. As you want, change the words in your definition to better suit your true definition of success. Many people will write it on a mirror, or on a Post-it note or as part of their daily journaling or planning process.

Step 5:

Revisit your definition of success on a quarterly basis to ensure it still fits your desires and is driving your goals and progress in business. Revise as needed.

(Optional) Additional Exercise:

If you're feeling stuck, this additional exercise can be helpful.

List out the things you want. An example of what this can look like is:

• $10,000 in savings

- a new car

- to create a website

- take BFFs on a trip

Next to each item, list why you want that item by asking, "What would it do for me if I achieved this?" An example of what this can look like is:

- $10,000 in savings = *so that* I feel security that I have money if an emergency came up

- a new car = *so that* I have safer transportation

- to create a website = *so that* I feel like I have a legitimate business

- take BFFs on a trip = *so that* I have quality time with friends and it allows me to treat them to something special

Remember, no answers are right or wrong with this; the exercise simply helps you know what your deeper desire is for each. Once you've written your "so that" statement next to each, look to find a common theme, so you can draft your success definition. Follow steps three to five.

As you go through this process of defining success as part of your Y.O.U. Promise, remember that this can change as you evolve and that done is better than perfect. Don't worry about writing it perfectly, just get it done so you can move forward.

KEY TAKEAWAYS:

- Defining success is part of the O in your Y.O.U. Promise.

- Goals are metrics we set in order to achieve success; they don't define success for us.

- Our definitions of success will change over time.

- As business owners we'll likely start with a financial focus and evolve later.

- Understanding our "so that" sentences will help define success.

RECOMMENDED ACTIONS:

1. Go through the step-by-step exercise outlined in this chapter on how to define success for yourself.

2. Revisit your definition on a quarterly basis after you've settled on a definition.

PART 3

UNAPOLOGETICALLY USE WHAT WORKS FOR YOU

Understanding what works best for you shows you how to achieve your definition of success.

CHAPTER 5

IDENTIFY YOUR BOUNDARIES

———

Now that you've defined success as part of your Y.O.U. Promise, and you have your destination point, it's time to figure out how to get there. My first recommendation for you is to identify boundaries needed to achieve success just like you would have parameters for any travel plans.

If you know the destination is the beach, and you need to pack warm-weather clothes, spending hours online shopping for coats or researching the routes to drive to the mountains wouldn't be wise. I realize this analogy may sound silly, but it's often what we do when we don't have boundaries in place.

For me, this looks like spending time on Instagram because it's fun, but since being present is part of my definition of success, I need to be cognizant of when I choose to scroll. While I'm sitting at a table with friends or family is not the best time to do this, yet it happens. My present mind is pulled to random things on Instagram while I'm waiting for someone to join a video call if I reach for my phone while I wait.

Understanding this led to boundaries with my phone. For example, I don't have my phone out during meals with friends or family, and I also put my phone across the room and flip it upside down during specific times of my workday (e.g., before and during calls).

I'm definitely not an expert on this topic, and I'm a constant work in progress, but I'm committed as I've seen the benefits of setting boundaries when it comes to how I work.

Before I was an entrepreneur, I was an employee. This experience taught me many things, and one of which is that I can be a workaholic. I'm a people pleaser by nature, and this led me to working endless hours trying to get it *all* done plus worrying if it would be good enough for those who I worked for. If I kept going at that pace, it could have meant serious health consequences, but unfortunately, I wasn't aware of this.

Fortunately, two amazing people in my life (my husband and my mom) actually sat me down and had an intervention with me. Picture this… I fly home to Florida, so we can go to a friend's wedding, and as I sit chatting in the living room where I grew up, two people who love me dearly said these words:

"Your health is suffering. If you keep going like this, you're going to end up in trouble."

They shared that it's great that I have a strong work-ethic and want to achieve great things, but it can't come at the expense of my mental and physical health. I knew they were right. I was addicted to working and wore the stressed-out-worker-bee badge of honor proudly.

Because of their support, I was able to take the first step toward healthier habits. At the time, I hadn't read any books about boundaries. I didn't sit down for hours and contemplate what boundaries needed to be set or deliberate for days on what the "perfect" words were for those boundaries. I simply decided, "I won't email people after work hours anymore," and this made a big impact.

I was still a great employee, a great boss, and very productive, but the one thing I didn't do was email people after work hours. To be clear, I absolutely worked after work hours sometimes, but I didn't respond to emails, and that made the biggest difference in the world!

I eventually turned in my notice at that job and worked at another corporation before starting my own company. It was in the next corporate job that I had the opportunity to start fresh and build stronger work-life integration habits.

In one job, I was crawling my way to burnout (with my badge of honor proudly showing), but in the other, I had found a better balance with what I needed in my life. That's the thing about boundaries; they don't have to lead to a big change to make a huge impact on your life. Had I attempted to change everything about my work habits at once, it likely wouldn't have worked. But instead, I changed one thing, and it had a ripple effect.

Because I wasn't emailing late at night, I was able to truly disconnect from work. This led to me leaving work at five o'clock instead of the late hours I was putting in at the previous company, and because of this, it was the start of a wonderful friendship. I found a new friend who lived close to me, and we ended up carpooling to and from work and even started attending a fitness class together after work.

What started as "I won't email people after work hours anymore" actually led to a new habit in my life of prioritizing my physical health. If that's not a win, I don't know what is.

I'm not alone in this pattern either; my friend and biz bestie, Kendi, reflected on her similar path when I interviewed her on this topic. She said that while she was climbing the corporate ladder she *"couldn't say no,"* and it led to a year of significant health issues that resulted in her exploring entrepreneurship, so she could *"create a working environment that allowed me to honor my unique boundaries... I was no longer willing to tolerate [lacking boundaries] once I understood that this was an option."*

If you just read "couldn't say no" and thought "yep, that's *me*," Kendi and I would like you to know that you're not alone and that you can learn how to implement boundaries. There's hope for us all.

HOW BOUNDARIES WORK FOR YOU

Just like there's a journey to defining success for yourself, the journey to discovering what boundaries you need in place as an Accidental Entrepreneur takes time as well. Learning more about what boundaries are and how they work can help kickstart your journey.

For example, a study was conducted to determine the effects of a fence around a playground and how it impacted children playing. The teacher took a class to one playground with no fence and observed how the children played and then at another time took them to a comparable playground that had a fence. This is what was found:

> In the first scenario, the children remained huddled around their teacher, fearful of leaving her sight; they didn't use the full playground space. The later scenario exhibited drastically different results, with the children feeling free to explore within the given boundaries. The overwhelming conclusion was with a given limitation, children felt safer to explore the playground. Without the fence, the children were not able to see a given boundary or limit and thus were more reluctant to leave their caregiver... The fence is a visible reminder that they are safe from harm *(KuneoDallas 2013)*.

If you're a visual learner, you can watch a short video demonstrating this study at amandamckinney.com/more

While the boundaries we will set for ourselves aren't visible like a fence, they serve the same purpose: to provide a limitation where we feel freedom to explore. This study opened my eyes to the idea that when we set boundaries, it actually increases our creativity within that space. It's not a restriction; it's an invitation to explore, and we absolutely need this as Accidental Entrepreneurs.

This could show up for you in business when you set time boundaries: "Time boundaries consist of how you manage your time, how you allow others to use your time, how you deal with favor requests, and how you structure your free time" (Tawwab 2016).

Yep. We definitely need to tackle this one because if you're anything like me, or anyone I've ever worked with, falling prey to Parkinson's Law is easy. Parkinson's Law states that "*work expands* so as to fill the time available for its completion" (*Economist* 1955). Meaning, whatever time we allow ourselves for a specific task, that's exactly how long the task will take.

I was working with a client of mine, Kim, who ran into this exact issue but didn't know it. She sent me this message:

"Help me, Amanda. It just took me three hours to record a three-minute video. Please tell me I can do something to make this better!"

My response to her was, "Yes, you can do something, and it's really simple. I need you to give yourself a time limit to record your next video, and I suggest ten minutes. Outline the points you want to make in the video, get yourself ready, and then set a timer for ten minutes. Record the video, and be done with it. Move on with your day."

Kim took this advice and was amazed at how quickly this tip worked for her. She used this system the very next day, and within ten minutes had a new video for her business. She was thrilled, and I was proud of her for taking action.

This is a great example of how you can use time boundaries in your business, but it's not the only example. You could declare that you won't work after five o'clock, or maybe you will not work on weekends, or maybe lunch away from work is your boundary. The key is that you decide what boundaries, what limitations you want to set in place (like the fence in the study) so that you can run and play within those limits.

Boundaries are limits people set in order to create a healthy sense of personal space. Boundaries can be physical or emotional in nature, and they help distinguish the desires, needs, and preferences of one person from another (Good Therapy 2017).

We set limits.

I don't know about you, but when the word boundary is used it's easy for me to immediately think of rules *others* have set…

"Don't spend more than _____."

"Only take your bike to the end of the road, but don't cross the road."

"You can't really charge that much."

"You should be using _____ in your business."

However, as an Accidental Entrepreneur who's on a mission to be unapologetic about chasing your definition of success, it's time to take control of who is setting the boundaries in your business. You get to set these limits, and even more, the person you'll need to set them for the most is often yourself.

When you set your own boundaries, you can protect what matters most, and set yourself up for success—the success you defined for yourself. Boundaries put you back in the driver's seat and can make all the difference in your life.

While I'm a work in progress on this topic, someone in my life inspires me with how she honors her boundaries and encourages others to do the same. My friend, Kendi is a licensed therapist, yoga teacher, and overall fantastic "boundary-setter-and-holder." (I hope she adds that new title to her website.)

I asked Kendi about her journey with boundaries because from my perspective, they came easy to her, and she was great at setting and holding them (#goals). But it was quite the surprise when Kendi laughed and said, "It was definitely learned… Entrepreneurship and boundaries have to coexist. You cannot have a successful business without being willing to learn about boundaries and find a way of being successful with boundaries with yourself and with others and with time."

The thing about things we practice and integrate into our lives, is they start to look easy, and people assume they always were easy for us. But like anything we are eventually good at, it often starts with the beginner mentality we talked about in the introduction. We have to be comfortable with being uncomfortable, so we can learn and practice and then find ease.

Kendi shared that like many of us, she wasn't taught to set or embrace boundaries, especially in the workforce. One thing that really stood out to me is when she said this about how she was brought up to view a career:

You get a job. You go to work every day. You don't ask questions. You don't negotiate. You do your job; you do it well. You come home and put food on the table, and you do it again, and you stay at that company forever. Work is to provide. Work isn't for fulfillment. Work isn't to be challenged. It isn't for a sense of purpose and meaning; it is for a paycheck and stability.

While a paycheck and stability are certainly great things and necessities in life, as an Accidental Entrepreneur, you're challenging the part about work not being for a sense of purpose or meaning. You're going against the norm and creating a career for yourself that not only provides a paycheck and stability but also a sense of purpose and fulfillment.

Anytime we set out to do something that's outside the norm or our typical way of doing things it's going to be met with resistance. This could be internal, where you're battling your habits and routines, or external, where you're battling others opinions or societal norms. Regardless, giving yourself grace as you navigate through this journey of setting boundaries is important.

AIM FOR WORK-LIFE INTEGRATION... NOT BALANCE

While you will set many more boundaries in place for your specific work-life integration, I feel especially passionate about the topic of time boundaries, and I want to expand on it. Throughout my experience as an entrepreneur and coaching other entrepreneurs, this comes up 100 percent of the time.

"I just don't have the time."

"Why does it take so long?"

"I can't fit it all into a day."

"I'm just so tired after trying to fit it all in."

For years now, I've read about "work-life balance," and it's never really sat well with me. One definition reads: "Work-life balance is the state of equilibrium where a person equally prioritizes the demands of one's career and the demands of one's personal life" (Sanfilippo 2023).

Don't get me wrong, I like the idea of work-life balance, and I've certainly aimed for this, but the whole idea that there will be a perfect balance of the two has never felt possible. There will be times when your personal life needs more attention than your work and vice versa.

Let's normalize building a business that integrates into your life instead of trying to balance it perfectly. And let's also normalize the fact that this is extremely difficult when you're passionate about the business you're creating.

Sometimes I'll find that I'm hard on myself for working on the weekend, but my supportive husband reminds me, "Amanda, you love what you do so when you work here and there on the weekends, it fills you up. As long as it doesn't take up all your time, don't worry about a few hours on the weekend if you really want to capture that idea or get something done. You love what you do, so it's adding to your life, not taking away from it."

As you're navigating this idea of boundaries for your time, keep in mind your work-life integration, and make it fit for you. You possibly have a full-time job, and this passion of yours is a side-gig at the moment. While the dream of having lots of flexibility with your schedule isn't a reality quite yet, you're working toward it, and just like our definition of success changes, our boundaries can change with different seasons of life too.

For example, when I first started my business, I was newly married and was adjusting to also adding the title of stepparent to my roles. At that time, neither kid was driving, and because I built my business to work at home, I volunteered for the role of pick-up and drop-off when the kids were at our house which meant that I couldn't be working sometimes. The flexibility allowed me this opportunity and gift of time with my step kids, but it only lasted a season until they started driving.

In another season, I had much more time available for work yet I needed tighter boundaries around my time, so I didn't slip into old habits. And then in another season of life when my husband and I were caretakers for my father-in-law, I needed much more flexibility with my calendar.

Each season brings gifts and challenges, but as an entrepreneur you're able to shift your boundaries with what your current needs are. We often don't have that luxury when we work for others, so once you step into this role, cherish this gift you have given yourself, and honor the boundaries that allow you to have the integration you desire.

Hear from my client, Pia, on this topic and how she went from feeling like her life had no room left for anything but work to finding a better work-life integration. She shares her "eight plus eight plus eight" formula in podcast episode #150 on *The Unapologetic Entrepreneur* podcast.

HOW TO SET YOUR BOUNDARIES

Do you like home renovating/decorating/organizing shows? I do, and I could watch this guilty pleasure all day. Some weekends, I actually do. One of my favorite things is to have a slow Saturday morning where I'm drinking my coffee, eating delicious breakfast, and watching home shows.

Just in case you aren't like me, here's how the home shows go:

- learn the backstory about the person/people in that episode

- see their messed-up house/room

- the hosts then share how they will help them

- see the plan for the updates

- reno/decorating/organizing starts

- some sort of issue is uncovered and then solved

- the big reveal at the end

I bring up home shows because as I was thinking about setting boundaries, two things occurred to me:

First, we usually uncover when we need boundaries after something happens, and we realize we don't want it to happen again. And second, before we identify the boundary, things feel messy and usually uncomfortable.

We're now at the point of the home show where you've seen the messy house. You've uncovered your mess, and it's not pleasant. So, I want to remind you that you're doing great, and I do not want you to beat yourself up for the mess, whatever it feels like for you right now.

You're doing the best you can with the information and experience you have right now. You'll do better tomorrow and again the next day. And like any home project, it's going to feel messy before it gets better. So, let's take all that crap out of the pantry, so we can figure out what's expired, what can be combined, and what will earn top spot in your newly organized pantry.

Step 1:

Revisit your Y.O.U. Promise that includes your why, values, and definition of success to have them clear in your mind as you start to identify boundaries. Also remind yourself throughout this exercise to be clear about what your boundaries need to be but also realistic with whatever season of life you're currently experiencing. You will cycle through different seasons, and your boundaries will likely need to change accordingly.

Y—why you want to be an entrepreneur

O—opportunity to define your values and success on your terms

U—unapologetically use what works for you

Step 2:

In response to your definition of success, ask yourself, "What boundaries do I need to put in place to achieve success?" Here are some questions that could potentially help you in this part of the exercise:

- What needs to change so I can prioritize my mental and physical health?

- Who do I want to work with?

- What am I no longer willing to tolerate?

Step 3:

Set your time boundaries if they weren't part of step 2. Here are some questions that will help with this part of the exercise:

- When do I want to work?

- When do I absolutely not want to work?

- How much do I need to work to meet my financial goals?

Step 4:

Anticipate and plan for resistance. While we don't want to constantly worry about what could happen, planning for what you know is most likely to happen is smart. Whether it's internal or external, what can you put into place to help you navigate the resistance? Here are some questions that will help with this part of the exercise:

- What habits do I have currently that could distract me from achieving success, and how can I put something in place to help me break this habit?

- If someone pushes back on my boundary, what can I say/do to relieve the pressure of the pushback?

Step 5:

Write your boundaries in an easily accessible place. This could be a note in your phone, a notebook, or wherever it feels comfortable for you to capture these thoughts. Since setting and holding boundaries is a process that takes time and patience, having a place to be able to go back to and write updates or notes is important.

Optional: Share your boundaries with someone (e.g., therapist, family member, or friend). As we set and honor boundaries, having support along the way is important. More on this in the next chapter.

Step 6:

On a quarterly basis, check in with your boundaries and rate yourself on a scale of one to five (one—not effective; five—very effective) on how effective you are at honoring your boundaries. Below are some recommended actions for each number on the scale.

One and two: Consider revising your boundary as it's likely not realistic for this season of life. You can often back the boundary down to make it more realistic. For example, if you notice that "not working after five o'clock" isn't realistic, change your boundary to six o'clock, and then reevaluate. However, sometimes it requires a different boundary altogether. For example, if "not accessing Instagram during the day" isn't happening for you, and it's still interfering with your progress, the updated boundary could be to "delete the Instagram app, and only reinstall on the weekends."

Three and four: Continue with the great work you're doing to honor this boundary. If you feel like an adjustment is needed, feel free to make it, but most likely you simply need to continue honoring this boundary.

Five: Celebrate! Being effective with boundaries takes a lot of effort, and this is something to be celebrated.

Ongoing Check-in Exercise:

Kendi also shared something with me that has impacted how I recognize stress, and it's my favorite way to know when I likely need to evaluate/set boundaries.

Our bodies have our backs. Our minds are the last ones to figure it out. Our minds are like, hell yeah. More money. Absolutely. More notoriety, absolutely. More speaking engagements. Yes. Sign me up. The mind is just like, gimme, gimme, gimme, gimme, gimme. And isn't really satisfied. You know, the finish line is ever changing when it comes to success, and the mind is just skipping forward. It's skipping forward and skipping forward, but the body has your back.

Your body has your back. That's powerful, but also hard to understand if you're not aware of your body's signals. This was me for most of my life; however, in the last few years, I've learned to be more aware of what my body is telling me.

For example, I've noticed that I feel stress in my lower back. It's a superpower I have now because I get a little twinge back there, and I know it's time to pump the brakes. And I figured this out by asking one, simple question every time I felt stressed:

Where can I physically feel the stress in my body right now?

I committed to asking myself that anytime I felt stressed, and it took several times before it clicked for me. But what I noticed was even if I couldn't say where I felt it, I noticed that I would start stretching my back or thinking, "I need a massage; my back hurts." Slowly, I recognized that specifically my lower back is my warning for stress. It's the first red flag, and the more often I'm able to notice that signal, the more often I'm able to set better boundaries and protect my health.

I don't know what your body signal is, but I promise if you start to pay attention you will notice it eventually. Once you identify your body's signal for stress, begin tracking when this comes up for you. I suggest keeping a digital or written note that you can add to easily. As you make notes you, will see a pattern and can then allow those patterns to inform your boundaries.

For example, if you notice you consistently experience your body's signal for stress when your schedule is packed with back to back meetings/appointments, then you know to give yourself more white space on your calendar, when possible. If it's not possible in this season of your life, then explore options of how you can offset this stress throughout the day.

Remember that as you identify boundaries to help you achieve your definition of success, this may feel messy, and it's easy to focus on the things you don't feel you've done well lately. This is typical and to be expected, so give yourself a lot of grace during this exercise so you can be realistic as you set your boundaries and celebrate as you make progress with them.

KEY TAKEAWAYS:

- Setting boundaries is part of the U of your Y.O.U. Promise.

- Entrepreneurship and boundaries have to coexist to reach success.

- Boundaries increase our creativity and give us freedom to explore.

- Setting and honoring boundaries is a learned skill that takes time, patience, and grace with yourself.

- Work-life integration is more realistic than work-life balance.

RECOMMENDED ACTIONS:

1. Follow the exercises outlined in this chapter.

2. Find additional resources on boundaries that can help support you as you set and honor your boundaries.

3. Check in with your boundaries during your quarterly check-in.

CHAPTER 6

FIND YOUR PEOPLE

———

Why is asking for help so hard?

Maybe you don't struggle with this, and if that's the case, please know that it is a gift, and I hope you cherish it. But if you just read that first sentence and immediately thought, "Ugh, I don't know," then this chapter is written especially with you in mind and you are definitely not alone.

People struggle to ask for help due to several common reasons. Some people may fear that asking for help would make them appear incompetent, weak, or inferior... Some people are concerned about being rejected, which can be embarrassing and painful. Others may be concerned about burdening and inconveniencing others (Witte 2022).

No matter what your primary reason is, exploring these thoughts as entrepreneurs is important because spoiler alert: We can't do it all, even when we wish we could. We need people in our lives to whom we can say, "I need your help," and they will be there. Let me set the stage for you for one of those times this happened to me...

I had been prepping for months to record video lessons to update a course I had at the time. I'd talked to previous clients and was sure of the content. I'd written the scripts for the lessons. I'd cleaned my office and prepped it for my "fancy camera," lights, and teleprompter. I picked out my outfit, did my hair and makeup, and was ready to record.

I had two days blocked to do all the recording, and after a cup of coffee and breakfast, it was go time. I set up the camera, sat at my beautifully decorated desk, smiled, and hit record. I recorded six video lessons over the course of five hours, checking between takes that all was looking good.

It was time to break for lunch, and I was so proud of how much of the content I was getting through. Look at me go! One-woman production crew over here, nailing it! Or so I thought…

Since I was taking a lunch break, I was careful to keep everything in the same place on my desk. I took the video card out of the camera, so I could start the upload of the lessons I had recorded. And then I saw it…

The video was out of focus.

Every minute of the five hours of content was out of focus and unusable. Completely unusable. To say I was devastated is an understatement. I was furious. I was upset. I was unsure of what to do, so I cried, and I yelled. I'm not proud of those moments that followed, but I let myself feel all the feelings that happened because they were present and in full swing.

Two lessons came out of this tech meltdown:

1. Simple and done is better than fancy, especially when it comes to technology.

2. Find your people, and reach out for support when you need it.

Fortunately for me, I have a support system that I could turn to at that moment, so I didn't have to navigate it completely alone. While I was proud to be that "one-woman production crew," there are multiple people on an actual production crew for a reason. And that reason is because doing all the things yourself is really freaking hard, especially when you get "fancy" with the tech.

After I calmed down, I reached out to those support systems. First was my husband Michael, and I didn't really have to reach out to him because he heard every minute of my meltdown. I told you; I yelled. He came in and calmly asked what was going on, and after I cry-splained the situation to him, he asked if I knew where the camera user manual was—smart man.

While he quickly became an expert at operating this camera, I turned to my other support system: my biz besties. These are my friends who also run businesses and understand the crap that comes along with the title of entrepreneur. And at this moment, the troops were called in.

I shared that message of "I need your help," and the support on the other side of this was truly remarkable. First, and most importantly, they listened and let me cry and be angry and unsure all at the same time. Then when it was time to share ideas, they did. Between my biz besties sharing encouragement and questions like "what can I take off your plate in the next few days so you can have more recording time this week" and Michael watching more YouTube clips than I probably even know, we figured it out.

I recorded all the videos again the following day, and I believe they were better because of the extra-compassion I had as I spoke. Since I was teaching about marketing, and that tends to be an uncomfortable and frustrating piece of entrepreneurship for many new business owners, I was able to relate in a very relevant way. The course went on to help hundreds of people kickstart their marketing with confidence, and for this I'm so grateful I didn't give up.

This one-woman-show needed her people. Reaching out for support didn't make me any less capable; it made me human, and I learned that these two things live together. I could be a confident one-woman-show *and* ask for support. One doesn't take away from the other.

Want to hear this story in real time? I recorded a podcast episode that night sitting on the floor in my closet near tears. I didn't know what the next day would bring, and I wanted to share the real-life moment with you. You can find it all in episode #81 of *The Unapologetic Entrepreneur*.

YOU ARE NOT ALONE

While my tech meltdown story is just one of the big ones that I could tell you about, I could tell you about hundreds of tiny moments, too. I love being an entrepreneur because of the independence it allows me, but loneliness comes with that independence if you don't find your people.

Over the years of coaching entrepreneurs, I've heard these comments or something similar many times:

- I feel like I'm on an island.

- Why does it feel so hard sometimes?

- I know I'm the only one who's struggling with _____.

- I feel confused with all the digital noise about what I should be doing.

Accidental Entrepreneurship can feel lonely because not only are you starting a business from scratch that many people in your life might not understand but you're also going about it differently. Many resources for new entrepreneurs are focused on doing whatever it takes to make your business work, but as someone who is trying to build a business that integrates into your life instead of taking over it, you're looking for a different path.

This doesn't mean you won't run into hard times, like my tech meltdown, and have to do whatever it takes to figure it out. Hard work is part of what you've signed up for, but instead of forcing yourself to make it happen, I'm suggesting that you lean on your support system to help you through it.

Doing hard things will always be hard, but when you have a good support system to provide positive reinforcement and a mental safety net, you can push through hard barriers. Whether those barriers are mental, physical, racial, cultural, technological, or otherwise, we will all hit something. Yet what helps us to push through whatever we encounter and get to the other side is our support system. We need this as a means of business survival as entrepreneurs.

According to data from the Bureau of Labor Statistics, as reported by Fundera, approximately 20 percent of small businesses fail within the first year. By the end of the second year, 30 percent of businesses will have failed. By the end of the fifth year, about half will have failed. And by the end of the decade, only 30 percent of businesses will remain—a 70 percent failure rate (Carter 2021).

Seventy percent! I know I don't want my, or your, business to fall into that category of a business that failed, so after reading this stat it's natural to want to know "what do successful businesses have in common?" and that's exactly where my research led me next.

Not to my surprise, the idea of finding people to support you was present in most lists I came across.

- "Surround yourself with people you trust" (Master-Class 2021).

- "Find a mentor" (Wynnberg 2020).

Research done by Leeds University is what really caught my attention:

> Prior entrepreneurship research shows that entrepreneurs' social networks are important for performance. A key resource in social networks is informal support through encouragement, empathy, closeness, familiarity etc. Studies of the economic downturn of 2008 showed that social ties lessened some of the negative business impacts. Entrepreneurs are actively increasing emotional support for each other, creating a more cohesive community. The impacts of a crisis can be traumatizing, but the entrepreneurial networks that people have access to can help to alleviate this trauma. Knowing that others are going through the same issues and listening to how they have tackled them helps (Williams 2020).

As we are all aware, the pandemic took a toll on us in many ways. Being separated from people and feeling the isolation not only affected us personally, but also professionally. This research taps into how having a support system as an entrepreneur actually helped alleviate some of the impacts of a global crisis.

This crosses over into our personal lives as well. As you're purposefully building a business that integrates into your life, the tough things we encounter in our personal lives will inevitably impact our business, so having the support needed to navigate these times is critical.

WHO YOU NEED, WHEN YOU NEED THEM, & HOW TO FIND THEM

Whenever I share about finding support in your business, I often hear concerns about personality types (introvert/extrovert), preferences (in-person/digital), or feeling competitive. Please know that connection to other entrepreneurs doesn't have to look like a traditional networking event that you dread; it can be your version of connecting, and it actually lessens competition.

As part of your Y.O.U. Promise, you've identified why being an Accidental Entrepreneur is important to you, your values, your definition of success, and the boundaries that will help you get there. You didn't think I would switch gears and tell you a cookie-cutter solution for connecting with others, did you?

No way. You get to do this your way, my friend.

While I love to get together several times a year with my biz besties, book an Airbnb for a long weekend, and do business planning, you could do this differently. Maybe you enjoy a shared Google Doc where you share updates as you can and connect through words on a page. Or you start a private Facebook group where you can ask questions and share wins.

The key is to know yourself and identify the ways you can connect with others that will support you in this journey of entrepreneurship. As you navigate the super rough, yet awesome, road of entrepreneurship, you're going to need many different people—some throughout your entire journey and some you will only need for a season.

Here is the list of people that I suggest:

- friends/family
- mentors
- coaches
- therapists
- biz besties

In each section I'll share why you need this type of person, when you need them in your journey, and how to find them.

FRIENDS & FAMILY

Why you need them: You have these people in your corner for all the big things in your life, so they will be there for you in this part too. This doesn't mean that every single family member or friend will support you along the way, but know who you can lean on for encouragement when you need it, advice when you need it, or just to lend a listening ear.

When you need them: You need them throughout the entire journey. Tell them early (like now) in your journey, and allow them to be the encouragement you need. These are the people that you will allow to see you cry and be at your worst, so you will want them throughout your entire journey.

How to find them: Their names are already popping into your mind as you read this. They are the first ones you call when you want to share something exciting. You won't have to search for these people; they are built-in already. Whether it's a single name or a list of people, it's not quantity that matters, it's quality.

MENTORS

Why you need them: By my definition, mentors are people who inspire and/or teach you, and you need both these things as an Accidental Entrepreneur.

When you need them: These will also be with you throughout your entire entrepreneurship journey and will evolve over time. You might need someone to help you learn about getting set up as a business at first, but then a few years down the road you need help hiring people in your business. You will likely always have mentors, but they will change over time.

How to find them: You can find these people in many places (books, podcasts, groups, etc.). That person you met at the coworking space that shared insights with you over a shared lunch—that's a mentor. The previous work colleague that took a look at your résumé when you needed it—that's a mentor.

Even more, some of my biggest mentors are those who don't even know my name. People like Mel Robbins and Brené Brown are incredibly inspiring and educational to me, but they don't know who I am. This is one that I think we get in our heads about and think, "I have to find a formal mentor," but really, it's often much more casual than that:

> "Super mentors help solve significant problems in your life… Start with the problem. Find people who can help you. Make it easy for them to help you" (Koester 2022).

COACHES

Why you need them: These are more formal relationships you have with someone who is actively coaching you. This might mean you are paying them for a specific type of coaching (e.g., marketing coach) or it's not paid but more formal in how you meet (e.g., monthly check-ins). While coaches certainly teach and advise you as you work together, the main reason many people hire a coach is for accountability in taking action in their business.

When you need them: Like mentors, coaches are wonderful to have throughout your entire journey; however, your needs will change throughout your journey. The key with this relationship is that you have found a person that you resonate with and have an agreement as to how they will help guide you in a particular stage of your business and what support they will provide to you.

How to find them: Do your research before hiring a coach. If possible, ask for recommendations from other Accidental Entrepreneurs you know. If that's not possible, I recommend consuming content created by the coach (blog posts, videos, social media content, low-priced offerings) to get a feel for their coaching/teaching style.

Another option is to book a consultation call with the coach. Whether the call is paid or free, it's a good idea to work with the coach for a short period of time (e.g., one hour) to understand how they show up for you as a coach before committing for a longer stretch.

THERAPISTS

Why you need them: I'm a big believer that everyone can benefit from therapy, and that extends to Accidental Entrepreneurship too. A therapist can help you navigate the tough times in life and business through conversation and helpful tools.

When you need them: Throughout your journey, but specifically if you're experiencing many stressful things in your personal and business life, that is a good time to have a therapist.

How to find them: Asking trusted friends or family members for recommendations is a great place to start. However, if this doesn't feel comfortable for you, an online search is a great tool. You can look locally if you prefer to meet with someone in person, or many options for online therapists are available.

BIZ BESTIES

Why you need them: As I mentioned in my tech meltdown story, your biz besties will be the people you call on when you need support on the tough days in business. Whether it's a tech issue, low sales, or an idea for something you want to offer, they are often the first line of defense. You may giggle when you read the title "biz bestie," or maybe it resonates with you. If you love it, use it. If you hate it, choose different words because the title doesn't matter—the people do.

Biz besties are people in your life that are also running businesses of their own, and they are willing to talk about the process, listen to you vent, celebrate with you, and help you problem solve, too. They become your friends over time but the thread that makes the biggest difference is that they are also running a business. If they aren't doing this, they can still be your BFFs, but they aren't "biz besties."

One of my biz besties, Shannon Crow, said it this way: "Have some entrepreneurial friends because if you have nine-to-fivers in your life or whatever shift they work, they are just not going to understand you."

When you need them: You need them throughout the entire journey yet these people will likely evolve over time in your business as these relationships take time to develop. These relationships are more likely to feel more settled a year or so into running your business although if it happens earlier, embrace it.

How to find them: The best mentality you can have with this process is to be the biz bestie you hope to find. Asking "how can I support you" is a great way to start as you begin connecting with people.

This is likely going to be the toughest group to find because it takes time. To find these people, you must be proactive in looking for other Accidental Entrepreneurs who are on a similar path. As you interact with others in online forums, group programs, memberships, or masterminds, see who you naturally connect with.

For example, if you're attending an event (local or online) and someone asks a question that you also have, connect with that person. Walk up to them after the event or send them a direct message; introduce yourself and thank them for asking such a great question. They will be thrilled they weren't the only one who was curious. Exchange contact information and then be proactive with connecting with them in the next few days.

Also, don't underestimate the power of social media. Many of my biz bestie relationships started by connecting on social media. This can look like engaging with or sharing someone else's content and then exchanging direct messages. What starts as a message can turn into a deep friendship one day.

This group of people is who I get the most questions about, so I wanted to share some additional notes:

- A magic number of how many you need does not exist; it could be one person or several.

- There is not a timeline for these relationships, but they do take time to develop.

- Start with messages back and forth, graduate to a coffee chat in person or over video, then ask, "How can I support you?" Then follow through with what you say you will do.

- Don't get discouraged if a connection doesn't lead to a biz bestie friendship; they don't all work out.

- Avoid jumping into a partnership or collaboration on a project right away; start small.

You will eventually say, "I wouldn't have the business I have today without them" about your biz besties, so it's worth the time and energy to invest into finding them.

COLLABORATION OVER COMPETITION, ALWAYS

The other thing I receive pushback on in this process of finding support is the idea of competition. The common fear I hear is, "I'm worried about connecting with someone who's doing something similar to me," but the real fear is "what if they steal my idea?"

Your fear is real, and I don't want to diminish that, but it's critical that you don't let this fear take over. Chances are they won't steal your idea because it takes effort to do that, but even if they do, they can't do it like you can.

I've had people blatantly copy my work, almost word for word, yet it didn't work for them because my personality and past experiences influence who I am as a coach and the work I put out into the world.

> I also worked with an attorney to help protect my work. See additional resources on this at amandamckinney.com/more.

You have the same advantage.

Let me say it this way, and I hope it really, really sinks in… Someone could offer the exact same product or service as you but the difference is *you*. For example:

- You could be a yoga teacher and teach the same class as someone else, but your words, playlist, and energy will be different. Just like you prefer specific teachers, others will prefer you.

- You could be an artist and even if you were commissioned to create the same work of art as someone else, it would turn out different, and someone would prefer yours over the other.

- You could be a writer penning a self-help book about entrepreneurship, but it will be different because you are writing from your own experiences and personality and have a unique voice of your own.

I want you to remember this the next time you feel that ping of competition. Pause whatever you're doing when you feel it creeping in, and assess what's going on. Almost every time it's because you're doubting your own business in some way, and if you can pause and remember your why and unique difference, this will help tremendously.

The go-to question to help with this is, "What differentiates my product/service from similar offerings?" From this answer you will feel more confident in moving forward.

Now it's time to find your people as part of your Y.O.U. Promise. Whether you want to call them your "team," "crew," "board of directors," or something completely different, it's up to you. Start with those who are already in your corner, and then allow that circle of support to expand into the other types of support.

KEY TAKEAWAYS:

- Identifying your support system is part of the U of the Y.O.U. Promise.

- A support system doesn't make you less capable on your own; it makes you human.

- Accidental Entrepreneurship can feel lonely, but it doesn't have to be.

- There are several groups of people you'll want in your corner during this journey.

- Finding your support system takes time, but it's worth the effort.

RECOMMENDED ACTIONS:

1. Identify your friends and family who are part of your support system.

2. Identify your mentors who are part of your support system.

3. Identify or start the process of finding your biz besties.

4. As needed, find the best coaches for you in your journey.

5. And all along the way, remember to utilize your support system instead of trying to do it all yourself.

CHAPTER 7

TAP INTO YOUR STRENGTHS

——

What are your strengths?

I know this can be a tough question to answer as we often overlook our strengths and focus on the things we see as weaknesses and want to fix. But as an Accidental Entrepreneur who's on a mission to build the business of your dreams, tapping into your natural strengths will provide more ease in your life overall.

For example, a strength of mine is breaking a project down into smaller pieces before it becomes overwhelming. I never would have thought of this as a strength because it's something I do naturally, but this has been pointed out to me many times in my life and especially as an entrepreneur.

While this strength helps me in life as I can reorganize an entire pantry without getting overwhelmed, it also helps me in business because I break down projects and actually get them done. This ability to break things down has allowed me to not just start projects but actually finish them and to do so in a way that feels easier for me.

Allowing your strengths to guide what you do and how you work as an entrepreneur will save you lots of frustration and time. But don't get me wrong, you won't love *everything* you have to do as an entrepreneur. If you think that's the case, it's time to take off the rose-colored glasses, but you can exchange them for rose-rimmed glasses. They can still be stylish… just with a more realistic lens.

So how can you identify your strengths? I've found four effective ways if you're struggling with this:

1. Tracking how you work and what's helpful

2. Personality assessments

3. Identifying your zone of genius

4. Understanding what helps you work best

TRACKING HOW YOU WORK
You know how the first step in budgeting is to look back at what you've spent over the past few months, or how the first step in understanding your caloric intake is to track what you're eating in a day? We're going to take the same approach to find your strengths.

By tracking your daily work habits and routines, you'll identify your strengths by finding what helps you make progress, and along the way you'll find what stops you from making progress, too. Both pieces of information are going to help you in your overall goal of creating the business that integrates into your life, but I also know it's tempting to want to skip this exercise.

It can be embarrassing, like accurately looking back at your bank account or your food diary. I get it because when I first started tracking my time, I was mortified too. But the first step is acknowledging reality, so you can make better decisions going forward.

> I have been using an app to track my time, and it has shown me much more about my productivity than I had even imagined. It has also helped me realize that my perception of how I spend my time is not remotely what I thought it was (Loucadoux 2021).

> I sometimes have productivity blinders in addition to my accomplishment amnesia. If something is hard, I assume it's a productive activity. If it's easy (like gardening), I assume it is not productive and subsequently vastly overestimate the time I spend doing it. That few minutes of gardening was a palate cleanser for my day. I was able to take a moment, go outside, reset, and restart. In fact, it probably made me more productive (Loucadoux 2021).

Tracking what you do with your day to see how you actually work can lead to insights on how you can be more productive, but it can also give you the permission you need to celebrate your progress and productivity.

Plus, tracking progress has many benefits as you're working toward something: "If you are trying to achieve a goal, the more often that you monitor your progress, the greater the likelihood that you will succeed, according to research. Your chances of success are even more likely if you report your progress publicly or physically record it" (American Psychological Association 2015).

Below are just five benefits of tracking:

1. The mere-measurement effect: measuring your activity will push you to do more/change (Morwitz and Fitzsimons 2008).

2. It establishes a baseline: it helps you understand where you are currently in relation to where you want to go.

3. It reminds you of progress: by tracking improvement/progress, you're able to celebrate along the way.

4. It identifies problems: it helps you see when you encounter a roadblock/lack of progress, so you can fix it faster.

5. It focuses your attention: even though it can feel like a chore at first, it helps you stay focused on what you want to accomplish.

While you can track your daily routine and habits in many ways, I found a free and easy-to-use tool when I started my business, and I still use it today. Toggl is the time tracker I use, and I love that it's a manual process because it makes you even more aware of your tendencies.

You have to open the app or go to the website to start the timer and tell it what you're doing. The best part is when you notice that in the middle of writing a blog post you pick up your phone instinctively to check a social media app or your email, you have to go to the timer and change what you're doing.

That's where the magic comes in! While you don't necessarily have to change the behavior in that moment, the simple act of having to change your entry can help you avoid the potential pitfall of what I like to call *procrastiworking*.

Procrastiworking is when you're doing something that could be considered work, so you feel justified in taking the action but it's definitely not the thing you need to be doing. It's you procrastinating by doing other work.

Here are some of my procrastiworking ways that were made evident to me:

- I wasted *way* too much time on Instagram.

- I love, love, love reverting to checking my email when I don't want to do something.

One of my clients shared with me that how she procrasitworks is by switching to an easier task. While it's not the task she needs to be focused on, she switches because it's easier for her, and she can cross it off her list. I have a feeling that you can relate to at least one of these examples, so no matter what's on the other side of your tracking, we all have things we will learn.

You'll have many aha moments as you begin tracking your time, but I think one of my favorite benefits that I've seen is how things change over time and actually improve. For example, when I first started tracking my time, it took an average of 1.5 hours for me to write, edit, and schedule an email, but now it takes less than thirty minutes. Talk about an improvement! But I never would have known if I didn't track my time.

PERSONALITY ASSESSMENTS

Another way you can identify your strengths is through taking personality assessments. While they aren't all created equal, and you wouldn't want to only rely on them, think about the fact that so many employers use these tools during the hiring process. They are trying to figure out if you will be a good fit for two things: the role and the team/culture.

So, I ask you this… if a potential employer can use these assessments to identify these things, why can't you use them to tap into your strengths as an entrepreneur?

You can.

Below are several personality/characteristic type assessments and how they are useful, but it really doesn't matter which or how many you look into. The key is to identify your natural strengths so that you can use those to your advantage as an Accidental Entrepreneur.

Ayurveda:

While not a personality assessment, this is something that I've seen entrepreneurs use to find the best work-life integration and navigate different seasons of the year.

Ayurveda translates to "knowledge of life." Based on the idea that disease is due to an imbalance or stress in a person's consciousness, Ayurveda encourages certain lifestyle interventions and natural therapies to regain a balance between the body, mind, spirit, and the environment (Johns Hopkins, n.d.).

CliftonStrengths (formerly StrengthsFinder):

This assessment solely focuses on your strengths and how you can optimize them in your work life.

Their website says, "Discover what you naturally do best, learn how to develop your greatest talents into strengths, and use your personalized results and reports to maximize your potential" (Gallup 2023).

Enneagram:

Each number has strengths, and while there are some numbers that tend to be more entrepreneurial by nature, all numbers have strengths that can be helpful as an Accidental Entrepreneur.

The Enneagram (Ennea=9, Gram=Diagram) outlines nine basic Personality Types that clearly describes why each of us thinks, feels, and behaves in particular ways based on our core fears and desires. This powerful tool can help us harness and transform self-limiting behaviors into life-enhancing personal empowerment (McCord 2019).

Human Design:

This one is different because this assessment is dictated by your birthday and few other facts, not answers to questions. You can use this assessment to find shortcuts to operating in a way that feels best for you.

> Human Design shows you a concrete map of your own nature and provides you with simple tools for making correct decisions, being yourself, and eliminating resistance in your life. Human Design offers you the opportunity to discover yourself and begin to understand and accept your very nature. Human Design uses your birth data to calculate your design chart, or Bodygraph, which determines your Type and Definition, the key components of the system (Human Design, n.d.).

Kolbe Index:

This assessment helps you understand your natural tendencies, so you avoid frustration as an entrepreneur. Once you know your instincts, you can play to them as strengths.

> The Kolbe A Index (Instinct Test) is unique. It does not measure intelligence, personality or social style. It measures the instinctive ways you take action when

you strive. Use your custom Kolbe A Index Results to be more productive, less stressed, and unlock joy at work or with your family (Kolbe Corp, n.d.).

Myers-Briggs:

In this assessment, you're assigned a set of letters that correlate to descriptors that can help you understand your strengths as well as how you work with others.

Specifically, "The Myers-Briggs Personality Type Indicator is a self-report inventory designed to identify a person's personality type, strengths, and preferences" (Cherry 2022).

YOUR ZONE OF GENIUS

Many people talk about the zone of genius, but my favorite definition I've read so far is:

The Zone of Genius is a place of flow, creativity, energy, and fulfillment. You lose your sense of time when you are doing activities in your genius. You love it that much! You would pay money to be able to do this all the time. Your success comes naturally when you do activities from your zone of genius. It feels effortless for you to do this. These activities give you energy, restore you, and fulfill you. You feel very present and are intrinsically motivated (Joyce 2021).

Isn't that awesome?

I think if everyone could do this and get paid, the world would be a much happier place. While I know we can't all do this, a select group of us out there are willing to give it a try. I call us Accidental Entrepreneurs.

What's your zone of genius? If you aren't sure yet, this could take time to unveil itself but, here are some questions to help you explore:

- What are you doing when you lose track of time?

- What's something you would love to get paid to do?

- What are some things that people tell you, "You make it look so easy"?

- What are some things that you feel come naturally to you?

- How do any of these things come into play as an entre-preneur? Or how could they?

Once you know your zone of genius, it doesn't mean you won't have to do other things as you're getting started, but knowing what you want to work toward is the key. For me, this looks like creating content that encourages and motivates people to actually take action. If I could simply create content (video, audio, written) and not touch the rest of my business, that would be me operating in my zone of genius.

I can't wait for the day I don't have to do things outside my zone of genius, but until then, I can make strategic decisions to stay in my zone as much as possible, and so can you. This can look like finding tools and software to help with things that fall outside your zone or even outsourcing to contractors/ freelancers.

As a coach for entrepreneurs, I'm asked about outsourcing, and this is my go-to answer: The things you want to outsource in your business, either today or down the road, are things outside your zone of genius.

WHAT HELPS YOU GET THINGS DONE

Think back to the last time you finished a project and ask yourself what really helped you get it done? Here are a few things I've heard from people I've worked with:

- deadlines

- to-do lists

- expectations from others

- keeping your word to yourself

Knowing what this is for you and truly stepping into whatever it is will help you get more things done. Sure, it's not healthy to always pull all-nighters for things, but if you know that you work well under a time deadline, then give yourself a fake deadline that you take seriously. Or if you know that you work well when someone else depends on you, then find an accountability buddy.

As I explored this about myself, here are a few things I noticed:

- Structure to a project helps me.

- I have the most concentration in the morning.

- Putting on 2000s hip hop music can turn my mood around for the better.

While these might seem like random facts, here's how they apply to my role as an entrepreneur:

- My love of structure has allowed me to start and finish projects on a timeline and keep my commitments.

- The fact that I know I concentrate best in the morning has helped me organize my day to maximize productivity.

- I've created specific playlists to shift my mood if I need a pick-me-up ASAP.

The key is to know the driving force for you when it comes to getting things done in your business. Once you know this, you have the key to unlocking your productivity that leads to success.

RECOGNIZE YOUR LIFE CIRCUMSTANCES/SEASON

Another component that's absolutely critical to acknowledge as you dive into learning how you work best is the season of life you're in. For example, while I definitely work best in the morning, there have been seasons when other areas of my life needed my morning time, so it wasn't available for my business. This didn't mean my business went down in flames, it just meant I had to use my other strengths more in that season.

I've cycled through several seasons since becoming an entrepreneur, and each one has its gifts and challenges. One summer I had more flexibility and enjoyed lots of time outside, but the next summer I had a very different experience. That's the other thing I've come to understand: Seasons in life don't show up routinely like the seasons of weather we experience.

Life seasons are much more unexpected.

I've experienced this personally and had the honor of getting a sneak peek behind the curtain of the lives of the entrepreneurs I've worked with. One thing is the same with almost every single person I've worked with: They are strapped for time.

I thought I understood as I was doing the same thing, wearing *all the hats* and trying to learn and do it all. But I didn't fully understand one speed bump until my husband and I moved his dad into our home to provide him care. I understood a lack of time (e.g., only five hours a week to work on your business) but I didn't understand how much interruptions kill the flow of work.

So here I am coaching people and saying, *"Set a timer for thirty minutes and write the email"* because I truly believe you don't need a lot of time to take action, you just need to do it. Well, I set my timer, and guess what I learned?

When someone (or something) else relies on you, that need doesn't wait for your timer to go off.

I learned that while my intention was good with the idea behind setting a timer and getting things done, that sometimes it's just not realistic. Your kid needs help getting something off the shelf. Your dog needs to be let outside. Your father-in-law needs something. Each time you help, it pulls you out of your groove.

Maybe you're in a season of life where this is your reality. If that's the case or if you run into this later, please remember to give yourself grace and that those seasons won't last forever. While you're experiencing a less-than-ideal schedule, you'll have to do things a little differently than you'd like to, but you can still get things done.

I would also tell you to remember that you're doing the best you can with what you have right now. That's the thing about entrepreneurship: we often think we have to have it all figured out, but the reality is that we do the best we can with what we know today, and we will repeat that tomorrow and the next day and the next day.

Know better, do better.

As you take the next step in your Y.O.U. Promise and identify your strengths, be sure to think about your strengths as a person first and then an entrepreneur. Doing our best to separate the two is easy, but if you can take your natural gifts and strengths and apply them to your Accidental Entrepreneurship journey, it will serve you better in the long run.

KEY TAKEAWAYS:

- Identifying your strengths is part of the U in your Y.O.U. Promise.

- Focusing on your strengths is more effective than trying to fix weaknesses.

- Tracking your time and work habits can help you be more productive.

- Personality assessments can help you as an Accidental Entrepreneur.

- Understanding your season of life will help you set yourself up for success.

RECOMMENDED ACTIONS:

1. Identify the season of life you're currently in and any limitations to your work schedule that you have. Setting yourself up for success by being realistic with your schedule and work routines is important.

2. Choose one method you'll use to identify your strengths (personality assessments or zone of genius). While you can choose multiple, focusing on one at a time is best.

3. Set up a system for tracking your daily habits, routines, and working time. This will allow you to see progress over time instead of a single moment in your life/business.

4. Based on the strengths you identified, how can you better use them to your advantage as an entrepreneur?

CHAPTER 8

FIND FINANCIAL CONFIDENCE

If we don't talk about finances, you just have an expensive hobby on your hands.

While hobbies are great, you're reading this book because you want to have a successful business, so talking about finances is critical. But before we dive into the good stuff, I should note that I'm not an accountant, financial planner, or attorney, so be sure to consult professionals on these topics beyond what I cover in this book.

What I am, however, is a fellow Accidental Entrepreneur who was terrified of the money-side of running a business yet navigated it with success and will share my lessons learned.

The most important things I've learned on this topic are:

- Take it one step at a time, and you'll be fine.
- Use resources from others.
- Know what enough is, financially.

TAKE IT ONE STEP AT A TIME

I'm not sure where you are with your financial competency, but when I started my business, I was very low on that scale of knowledge and confidence. While I had worked with large budgets in my corporate days, I was very nervous about anything that related to overall financial forecasting and taxes.

I had been telling myself this story my entire life: "I'm bad at math." It started in school when I struggled with the subject and was perpetuated in adulthood as I had struggles with budgeting. I read lots of books and worked hard to learn how to not only budget for my personal life but to set myself up for future success through investing.

No matter how well I was doing with money, this story I told myself rang true in my mind, and it showed up in big ways when I started my business. Mainly, I didn't believe that I could run a company and felt that I had to hire someone to help me with anything that related to money.

As you know, money is tight when you're starting a company, and I didn't want to go into debt so I was faced with the reality of a choice. I either hired a bookkeeper with money I didn't have, which would put me in debt, or I learned how to do the bookkeeping on my own. Either option would have worked, but I chose to dive in and learn.

If you're curious how I decided which was best for me, it comes back to your Y.O.U. Promise which contains keys to your decision making. For example, one of my values is independence, and while it's defined as one thing for my business, another element is personal.

Personally, independence also means that I'm not in debt to anyone else financially or otherwise. I recognize that this isn't how everyone works, so I'm not saying I'm right, but for me, the decision was actually easy. If I hired someone, I would be going against one of my personal core values, and since it wasn't absolutely necessary in order to move forward, I chose to learn about monthly bookkeeping in business.

When you find yourself in a place to make a choice about finances or anything in business, go back to your Y.O.U. Promise and you'll have guidance immediately.

This brings me back to taking it one step at a time. Had I focused on the many financial tasks I would or might have to take on as an Accidental Entrepreneur, I could have been paralyzed with fear and doubt, yet taking it one decision at a time is what got me through this process.

First, I learned about simple monthly budgeting for businesses. Then I created spreadsheets to help me track the monthly numbers of what was coming in and what was going out of the business. Then as my business grew and needs changed, I learned more about businesses finances.

Over time, I became more confident in my business finances, and through that, I grew more confident as an Accidental Entrepreneur. Being debt free in my business and also paying myself are two things I'm very confident in today, but it took me learning and taking action to uncover my financial confidence. This came from finding helpful resources and learning from others.

I highly recommend working with a financial planner. Most people think financial planners are only for those with a lot of money or investments, but you can start today with whatever amount you have. Ask your friends or family for recommendations, or search for a financial planner local to you.

LEARN FROM OTHERS & USE RESOURCES

As I searched online for resources to learn from, I noticed two different types that were helpful when it came to finances: software and people. The software can help you automate things to help save time and energy, and the people can help you understand the process that works best for you.

Business Financial Systems & Software

This is where I see most new Accidental Entrepreneurs spending the most time, and it's probably because as soon as you google something about entrepreneurship, you start getting ads for these services. The key to remember is that all you need to do is pick a bookkeeping service that works for you. The system doesn't matter; what matters is that you feel comfortable and confident using that system.

Many options are available for entrepreneurs, and you can find them by searching for "bookkeeping software for small businesses." Once you find options, here is a list of qualifications that you can start with to ensure that you pick the best system for you:

- Does the software work with your country's currency?

- Will you be accepting multiple currencies? If so, does the system allow for that?

- Does the software connect to your banking and/or credit card institutions easily?

- Does the fee to use the software align with your budget?

- Will you need to send invoices to customers? If so, can you send invoices with this software? If so, is it easy for you?

- Will you be selling digital offerings? If so, does the software integrate with your delivery system easily?

- How do you like the interface of the software after you try it out for a bit?

My suggestion is to use the software's free trial to get a feel for the overall experience. Set up your products/services, send an invoice to yourself for one dollar, and pay it to experience the entire process. The goal is to walk through the process and see how you like the software and how it will feel for your customers to interact with it as well.

Another thing to note is that you might not have all your products or services figured out yet, and that's okay. Just like everything else in your business, this will likely evolve, and you might need to make changes down the road. You don't have to have it all figured out today because things (and software) can evolve throughout the process.

Business Budgeting & Processes

Just like many options for software exist, even more coaches and teachers online can help you understand your business finances. Please research this on your own, and use what resonates the most with you, but I have a go-to resource that I highly recommend.

Each quarter I receive a message that says something like this: "Amanda, thank you for encouraging me to use Profit First; I just paid myself a bonus, and I wouldn't have been able to do that without you sharing this method with me."

Profit First is a method created by Mike Michalowicz, and I've used this method since I started my business in 2017 (Michalowicz 2017). After listening to him on a podcast as I was driving, I pulled into a parking lot and paid myself one hundred dollars. That was my first paycheck, and I've paid myself every month since.

This method goes beyond paying yourself and is a process for your bookkeeping and budgeting all in one. By implementing this method, you will be set up to track everything financial in your business and ultimately be set up for financial health.

Profit First Method Overview:

Mike created this concept because he had some rough times with money and doesn't want you and your business to run into the same issue. He shares a story about his daughter bringing him a piggy bank with money to help him out, and from that moment on, he committed to doing money differently.

He created this system, and he says it's built for humans because humans are emotional, not logical, and in general, we will spend money if we have it. So, the idea is that we won't have a profit if we use it all for expenses. So, we need to take profit first.

Traditional business math says this:

Sales - Expenses = Profit

Profit First business math says this:

Sales - Profit = Expenses

Did you catch that? By using this method your expenses are less likely to get away from you because you're not taking them out first. Genius.

The monthly process is simple too. Each month on the tenth and twenty-fifth you do your bookkeeping sessions, so you always have a pulse on the financial health of your business. During these bookkeeping sessions you will track the income and expenses happening, pay any bills you have, and pay yourself. That's right my friend: you will pay yourself.

By doing business math the Mike-way, you will limit your expenses to what you can actually afford in your business, pay yourself, and always know your business' financial health. And you know what this does? It uncovers even more confidence in yourself as an Accidental Entrepreneur. Just imagine if the next time someone asked, "How's business?" you could confidently share that your business is debt free and profitable. You can, and you will.

Action creates confidence every time. My confidence in my budgeting didn't happen on day one after I made my first budget spreadsheet, and neither will yours, but it will grow over time. With each month you will get better with understanding your finances which leads to overall confidence.

Business Taxes

I couldn't talk about business finances without sharing about taxes, even though you probably want to skip this part... unless you're a tax accountant. And if that's the case, please open your business to help entrepreneurs with taxes because we all need you.

If you're like the rest of us, this is the part that scares the pants off you. Taxes can feel surprisingly scary to an Accidental Entrepreneur, and I wish I had some magic words that would make that fear go away, but I don't. What I do have though is proof that even if you're scared, you can still do this because I did, and so many others have too.

First, make sure you get your business entity set up, so your business is legal. For most of us, that will mean an LLC (limited liability company) or the equivalent in other countries outside the US, where I'm located. Once you have your business entity set up, you are now ready to work with anything tax related as well.

Consult with an attorney if you have questions
regarding setting up your business entity.

Remember that bookkeeping software you picked out? It's
actually going to help you prep for your taxes each year,
too. Once you have your banking information connected,
it will track your income, you will enter in some personal
information about how you file taxes, and then each quarter,
the software will tell you how much you owe in taxes. It's
like magic.

On this note, I highly recommend making estimated quarterly payments for taxes, so they don't creep up on you each
year. And if you take my other advice and use the Profit First
method, you will be set. I actually hear some version of this
every single year from my clients:

> Amanda, thank you for sharing Profit First with me.
> This is the first year I've ever been excited to pay my
> taxes because the money is just sitting there wait-
> ing for it to happen. Using this has helped lower the
> burden and worry about taxes so much.

That could be you next quarter.

KNOW WHAT ENOUGH IS FINANCIALLY

One of the main ways that I became more confident in my
business finances was truly understanding what enough
was for me. If you're not careful, you can fall into the trap

of always wanting more. More sales, more money, more followers, more, more, more.

Earlier, we talked about boundaries: Our brains will encourage us to want more, but we have to know our needs. This goes beyond your boundaries and into your finances, too, so knowing what enough is for you is essential, even if your ultimate goal is to make more than "enough." The great news is that figuring out what this is for you is very simple.

Step 1:

Identify if you need to bring in money from your business into your personal finances. This will differ for everyone and sometimes differs depending on the season of your life. For example, you may have a full-time job currently, so your needs are met financially, but your goal is to start your business now as a side gig.

Regardless of your situation, knowing if your business income is necessary or a nice-to-have bucket of money is important.

Step 2:

Identify exactly how much money is needed from your business to fuel your personal expenses (if needed) and your business expenses. This *must not* be a round number that you're guessing at, but an exact number based on expenses. For example, $1,114.99.

You get to this number by adding up all expenses that your business incurs currently, and add in your salary if you do need to bring in money to your personal finances.

Example:

- website software = $30 per month

- email software = $29.99 per month

- accounting software = $15 per month

- educational materials = $40 per month

- personal salary = $1,000 per month

Total = $1,114.99 per month

Step 3:

Factor in that you will not personally receive 100 percent of the revenue from your business and identify how much money you need to bring into your business to pay all the bills, including your salary.

If you use the Profit First method, you will get more detailed with this, but for the sake of this example let's assume you can bring home 50 percent of your business revenue as your owner's pay.

(Owner's pay x 2 + operating expenses)

$1,000.00 x 2 = $2,000.00 + 114.99 = $2,114.99

This means that if you bring in $2,114.99 per month in your business, you will be making *enough*. Most often when I work with people on this, it reveals that the "enough" number is lower than they thought it would be, and that's an encouraging moment.

You can also strive for more than your enough number, but knowing what enough is will keep you grounded so you're not on the *I-always-need-more* hamster wheel.

(Optional) Step 4:

If you're looking to eventually quit your current full-time job and are curious how to work through this math, you can go about this in two ways.

Option 1: Save and create a financial cushion to fall back on before quitting.

This simply means you build up a savings account to an amount that you're comfortable with and then you leave your job. Everyone will have a different comfort level but, if you go this route, I would suggest six months of income.

Example:

- your personal monthly financial need is = $4,256.76

- six months' cushion = $25,540.56

Meaning you would want to have a savings account with $25,540.56 at a minimum before you put in your two weeks' notice at your full-time job.

Option 2: Build up business first.

This is when you work on your side gig on nights and weekends until you can cover your monthly needs. Using the same example from above, you wouldn't put in your two weeks' notice until you were earning $8,513.52 in your business. This accounts for you being able to take home 50 percent of the business revenue as your owner's pay.

In your journey of showing up unapologetically as an Accidental Entrepreneur, financial confidence is a critical part. By understanding what enough is for your business and finding the resources that resonate most with you, you will be in a better place to show up confident in your finances.

As you identify these pieces of your Y.O.U. Promise, be sure to take it one step at a time as finances can be one area that becomes overwhelming, quickly. This is also a great topic to bring up with your support system when you're feeling unsure or confused. Most of the time when we can talk it out with someone else, we can work through the overwhelming feelings, and then take action.

KEY TAKEAWAYS:

- Understanding your finances is part of the U in your Y.O.U. Promise.

- Gaining confidence with your business finances will increase your confidence overall.

- The best way to learn about business budgeting and taxes is one step at a time.

- The best accounting/bookkeeping software is the one you can actually use.

- You can work with a financial planner no matter how much money you have in the bank.

RECOMMENDED ACTIONS:

1. Identify what enough is for you in business in this season of your Accidental Entrepreneurship journey.

2. Choose a financial software to use in your business.

3. Purchase *Profit First* by Mike Michalowicz, read the book, and begin implementing his process.

4. Find additional financial resources that will support what you need in your financial journey. I highly recommend working with a financial planner.

CHAPTER 9

SET REALISTIC GOALS

———

How do you cure hiccups?

For me it's eight tiny sips. I take eight tiny sips and swallow each sip and, bingo, the hiccups are gone. I've heard of so many ways to get rid of hiccups, and I've never known anyone else that "eight tiny sips" works for. I don't remember where I heard it or how long I've been using it, but it works, and I swear by it.

I bet you have something that works for you too. Whatever it is, you have your go-to method that works for you. Maybe you've even told other people about it and watched them try it, and it didn't work. But it works for you every time (or almost every time).

Why do you think that is?

I think it works because we believe it works. At some point you were willing to try something, and when it worked, you then believed. Even if I have to do my "eight tiny sips" method four times before it works, I will keep going because I know it will work the "next time." I have complete faith in this method, and I want you to believe in yourself like you believe in your cure for hiccups. No matter how many times it takes, no matter how silly you look, you're willing to do it because you believe in it. You believe in yourself.

While I in no way think that simply the belief in yourself will magically make your dreams come true (wouldn't that be nice!), I do believe it's a critical part of the equation.

Belief + Action = Progress

Just like it took once for your hiccup cure to work, and then you had confidence and belief in that method, the same will be true for your business-related confidence. As you make progress and recognize that progress, it will uncover more and more of your confidence.

When you believe in your ability to reach your goal and take action toward that goal, I promise with 100 percent certainty that you will make progress. I won't promise that you will achieve your original goal, but I promise you will make progress which will lead you to your destination of success over time.

In chapter 4 you learned the steps of how to define success for yourself, and I called attention to the difference between your success definition and your goals.

Success = the destination you're going toward

Goals = the milestones we set to achieve our definition of success

Now it's time to dig into goals so that you can start setting more realistic milestones for yourself and your business.

WHAT IS A GOAL?

Goals are "the end toward which effort is directed" (Merriam-Webster 2023).

Did you catch that? "Effort" is actually in the definition of the word goals. I think this is often missed because we set a goal and sometimes just *hope* it happens. I believe that "effort" in this definition often means "new or different effort," and that also means discomfort. Doing something new or different isn't always comfortable and is almost always not the easiest path, but it is often necessary.

Now that you know a goal will require effort and that it's the end toward which that effort is being directed, what's your end? Where are you currently applying your effort? If you're anything like me, sometimes those two things lead to different answers. For example:

Goal = to be healthier

Effort = no changes to diet or movement throughout the day

Goal = to make more money per month

Effort = same daily business routine

In both scenarios, the effort doesn't match the end results I'm trying to get to. I bet this has happened (or is happening) to you too because changing what you're already doing is really hard. Change is hard.

This is where your boundaries, strengths, and support system come into play. As you set goals, checking in with your boundaries and possibly adding in more is important. For example, if you want to make more money in your business and you recognize that you've been spending more time on social media lately with little return on your investment (you know this because you're tracking your time), you could set a new boundary of a social media time limit.

All the elements you've defined in your Y.O.U. Promise will help you as you strive to achieve a goal if you allow them to. I mention this because doing what you're doing is easier than making a change, but the work you're doing to set a strong foundation as an Accidental Entrepreneur provides the keys to your success.

Change is hard, but because you're learning more about yourself and what you're striving to accomplish, you have what you need to navigate hard changes.

SETTING REALISTIC NINETY-DAY GOALS

A goal is different from a realistic goal, and this is the key to achieving your definition of success. You've likely set many goals in your life, many of which stay in the graveyard of unmet goals, not because you didn't want to achieve it but because you actually couldn't achieve it.

We are typically great at setting goals and saying them to others, but we fall short with setting a *realistic* goal. This is because we often overestimate what we can do in a set time. Bill Gates famously said, "Most people overestimate what they can do in one year and underestimate what they can do in ten years" (Brown 2019).

Oh how true that statement is. I think I can take on the world in the next twelve months, but if you ask me what my ten year goal is, it wouldn't be much bigger than my one year goal. Our minds just don't think that way, and that's why I like the idea of ninety-day goals.

Since implementing this process for myself and also teaching others, I've come up with a simple process that you can do with a pen and paper.

Or you can use the free workbook that includes this exercise at amandamckinney.com/more.

Step 1:

Reflect on the previous ninety days, and list what you've been able to accomplish. Maybe it was one project, or maybe it was a bunch of tiny things. The purpose is to understand accurately what you were able to get done in the past ninety days. Notice where your effort was and what you accomplished.

Step 2:

Look ahead to see how many working days you actually have in the next ninety days because—spoiler alert—you don't actually have ninety days. Take out weekends, vacations, holidays, doctor appointments, etc., so you have an accurate picture of how many working days you have to work toward your goal.

Step 3:

Identify how many hours you typically spend working on your business in an average week. For example, if you work on your side-hustle five hours a week right now, and you realistically have ten working weeks in the next ninety days, that's a total of fifty hours of work time.

Step 4:

Remind yourself of your definition of success. From that definition, ask yourself, "How can my business contribute to this definition of success?" For example, let's say you're passionate about teaching yoga, and your definition of success includes traveling the world, your business could help you do this by providing revenue while being able to work from anywhere.

Step 5:

With that in mind, ask yourself, "What can I realistically accomplish in the next ninety days that will get me one step closer to my definition of success?" In the hourly example, you would ask, "What can I realistically accomplish in fifty hours of work time over the next ninety days?"

In the success example of traveling the world, something you could do in roughly fifty hours could be to create a list of yoga retreat locations and contact each one to do research on what type of retreats work best at their locations. This market research will set you up for more success than if you created a yoga retreat with no insight.

Your answer to, "What is something I can realistically accomplish in the next ninety days that will get me one step closer to my definition of success?" becomes your ninety-day goal.

I hope that you just had an aha moment like so many of my clients have when I walk through this process because this is game changing. Not just setting a goal matters; setting a realistic goal that you have a strong connection to matters.

This process of setting realistic ninety-day goals takes time, and you're most likely going to miss the mark the first few times. Remember, we often overestimate what we can do in a short amount of time, so your first few ninety-day goals might be unachievable, but the more you use this method, the better you will get at setting realistic goals.

I'll share more on why this is the case when we talk about tracking your goals later in this chapter, but first, we should talk about what's most likely to stop this process.

FEAR CAN STOP YOU

While we can point to circumstances, lack of something, or many other things when it comes to not achieving our goals, fear is most likely the main culprit. This isn't to say that other things don't get in the way as they are real and impact how we can make progress, but a thread of fear is often weaved in when it comes to Accidental Entrepreneurship.

I see three fears in myself as well as all Accidental Entrepreneurs I've coached:

1. What if it doesn't work?

2. What if it does work?

3. What will others think?

The common denominator in all of these is that we are focused on ourselves when we feel fear. However, if we can shift our minds from ourselves to how we are helping others through our business, we can then push through the fear.

What if it doesn't work?

We often say we are afraid of failing, but I believe that we aren't actually fearful of failure, but rather, we are afraid of others seeing us fail when it comes to Accidental Entrepreneurship.

Somewhere along our life journey someone made fun of us trying something new, and we realized that people laugh at us when we look silly. Maybe it was athletics, maybe it was a spelling bee, maybe it was something else for you, but the story is the same: you were a beginner, someone made fun of you, and your brain remembered that as a protection mechanism.

This is what stops you from taking your creative idea that feels fun and exciting and starting a business. If you say something is "just a hobby" then the pressure is off, but as soon as you say it's a business, things change. And if you don't have people surrounding you, lifting you up, believing in you, cheering you on, you will stop because your brain will tell you, "danger, someone might make fun of you for trying this" or "what if it doesn't work out?"

The reality of this fear is that most things you try as an Accidental Entrepreneur won't work, but if your why is strong enough, you'll keep going. I suggest that you combat this fear with this statement: "I trust my resources."

You're reading this book today because you are alive, and you've likely navigated some really hard things in your life that definitely didn't work out like you thought it would. Maybe you lost a job, didn't land the interview, went through a divorce or break up that truly devastated you, navigated a health issue, suffered the death of a loved one. This list could go on and on because there isn't one human being that hasn't suffered something hard. But you made it through because you used your resources, and you will do the same as an Accidental Entrepreneur.

What if it does work?

This fear relates to the fact that we typically don't like change, and if something does work out, things will likely change. One client of mine told me that she's often worried about her business growing and it taking time away from her kids, which is part of her definition of success.

Change is hard, but the beauty of creating your Y.O.U. Promise is identifying what matters to you so that you can control a lot of the change. In my client's example, she can monitor her time to ensure she doesn't go against her boundary of spending time with her kids because she is in control of her schedule.

I suggest combating this fear by using quarterly check-in points and reminding yourself that you can make decisions that help you navigate the change as it's happening.

What will others think?

This is the biggie. We are so dang fearful about what others are going to think about what we're doing or not doing that it paralyzes us from doing what we want to do. This happens in everyday life, like when we really want to wear that romper but are worried what so-and-so will say or think about it, but it really creeps in when someone thinks about taking a hobby/passion from an idea into a business.

The conversations with family and friends are often the most nerve-wracking. You could attend an event and share, "I'm starting an organizing business" with a stranger with ease, but when it comes to telling your cousin, it's terrifying. Most of the time these fears are in our minds, and while our friends and family might not understand the business you want to create (hello any online business!) or understand why you want to try, they will be supportive.

However, I know there are times when we have people in our lives that are less-than-supportive too. Their words will sting at first, but the way to combat this is to have your support system in place and limit what you share with others. If you know that your Aunt Sally is always negative, don't talk to her about your business at the next holiday gathering. If she asks you about it (which is doubtful), let her know you're excited about your business and how things are moving forward, and tell her you appreciate her asking. Then move the conversation to her because chances are she loves talking about herself, so you will successfully change the conversation with ease.

Sometimes we worry about another group of people more than friends and family, and that's "people on the internet." I get asked, "Amanda, how do you deal with mean people online?" often, and it tells me that we all worry about this. Here's the reality:

The more you put yourself "out there," the more chances you have for people to share their opinions which can be positive or negative, but in the beginning stages of business it's pretty manageable which gives you time to uncover your confidence. You might get an email from an unhappy customer or someone who doesn't agree with your thoughts on something, but most people won't really say anything.

I remember the first time I received an "I want a refund" email. My heart stopped, my stomach dropped, and then I immediately got super defensive, but only in my mind, thankfully. My defensive thoughts were really me being very upset. I thought I had failed; I *knew* I had failed.

Instead of drafting my response right away, I walked away from my computer and did other things. I remember thinking how upset I was, but my goal is to help people so after lots of reflection, I came up with something along these lines in response:

I'm so sorry that you're unhappy as that is the last thing I wanted when I created this course. I want to help you accomplish what you hoped to achieve. Please share your goal with me, and I will get back to you with my suggestions and any resources that can help you.

I went on to help that person through email and video responses back and forth all the while learning one of the biggest lessons that would carry me through entrepreneurship:

When someone is open with their criticism, you can improve upon your product. Welcome helpful feedback, always.

From that day forward, I have welcomed criticism and feedback in everything I do. Does it sting sometimes? Absolutely. But it has helped me improve on everything I've ever offered in my business, including the words in this book.

To combat the fear of what others will say or think, I suggest running the fear through these filters:

- Did the person actually say something or am I anticipating what they will say? If you're anticipating it, do your best to push the fear aside and take action because they may never say or think what you're worried about.

- Is this person a current or potential student/client/customer? If not, remind yourself that if they don't pay your bills, not paying attention is often best. This may sound harsh, but as an Accidental Entrepreneur who's following your passion, you should remember that your job is not to please everyone, it's to serve your specific audience.

- Is this something I truly believe in? If so, this is your moment to be unapologetic about what you stand for, and create in your business, no matter what others think.

Remember, you can take action and be scared at the same time. The goal isn't not to be fearful; it's to take action on what truly matters to you, so you can build the life and business of your dreams.

> Fear and excitement are the exact same physical state. Your heart races, you might sweat a little bit, you might feel tightening in your chest, you might feel a pit in your stomach, you have a surge of cortisol. It's basically how your body goes into a hyper-aware state because it's ready for action... The only difference between fear and excitement is what your brain is doing as your body is all agitated. If you're excited, your brain is saying, "Oh wow, this is going to be so cool," but if you're afraid your brain is saying, "Oh, no way" (Robbins 2017).

In those moments of fear, which will inevitably happen, take a deep breath, and do your best to shift your mindset to being excited. Since I know this is easier said than done, here are a few mindset switching affirmations for you to use if they're helpful for you:

- I'm scared it won't work = I'm excited to try something new even if it doesn't work out the way I think it will.

- I'm scared it will work = I'm excited to see what happens next, and know I can take it slowly if needed.

- I'm scared of what they will say = I'm excited to share what I believe even if others think differently.

I encourage you to write these or your own version in a place where you can see them when you need them. Fears are going to pop up as you're showing up in this new way in your life, and the more tools you have to navigate them, the better.

TRACKING YOUR GOAL PROGRESS

In addition to preparing for the fears that could stop you, you can track your progress. This is a tactical tool that will also be incredibly helpful. Just like tracking your time will help you uncover how you work best and allow you for more productivity, tracking your progress toward a goal will help you stay motivated.

I tested this idea, and as soon as I realized how powerful this exercise is, I immediately implemented it with my clients in a system called "progress logs." Here's how it works:

Each week you track your progress in a progress log.

Yep, that's it! That's the rocket-science I've come up with, and I hope you just giggled at how ridiculously simple this is because that was the point. So often we feel we need the newest software or tool in order to "level up" in business, but more often than not, the answer is as simple as this.

I suggest that my clients record answers to one or more of these questions each week in their progress log which can be kept in a digital document, a spreadsheet, a form, or whatever works for you. I do encourage that it's digital; how many times have you lost a notebook? Plus, you can search digital documents which makes it really neat too.

Questions For Your Progress Log:

- What have you accomplished this week?

- What got in your way this week? (roadblocks / setbacks)

- What did you learn this week?

Then each quarter, go back and review your log. During your review time, you will learn even more about yourself and how you work. From this review you're able to set even more realistic goals as you move forward, plus you get to celebrate your progress. Regardless of whether you hit your goal or not, you will have made progress and learned about yourself along the way. This is huge!

Being very honest with yourself is the key to this exercise because that will help you learn the most. Upon reflection of my own progress logs, I've been able to learn that walks in the middle of the day are very helpful for my productivity, Instagram is not essential for my business to make revenue, and the week before I launch anything tends to be more stressful. By learning these things, I can now plan better in my business and prepare my family for when I need some extra grace and patience.

You've set your destination of success, and your goals will help you get there, but remembering this is a journey is key. Just like we encounter detours when we travel, you'll experience tough times as you stretch yourself to reach new levels in your business. But allow your ninety-day goal to be your GPS and your progress logs to be a travel guide along the way so that you can enjoy the journey.

KEY TAKEAWAYS:

- Setting ninety-day goals is part of the U in your Y.O.U. Promise.

- Goals are the milestones we set to achieve our definition of success.

- You don't actually have ninety days to achieve a ninety-day goal.

- Fear and excitement show up the same in our body, and you can use this to your advantage.

- Tracking progress in a progress log will help you stay motivated.

RECOMMENDED ACTIONS:

1. Follow the steps to set your ninety-day goal.

2. Create your system for tracking progress in your progress log.

3. Review your progress log on a quarterly basis, so you can continue to learn more about yourself as an entrepreneur.

CONCLUSION

I hope you've uncovered more confidence in yourself than you even knew was there by creating your Y.O.U. Promise, and that you're ready to unapologetically chase your definition of success as an Accidental Entrepreneur.

You've been inspired through stories and examples, and I've laid out the step by step plan for you, but now it's time to take action and create your Y.O.U Promise if you haven't already.

Y—why you want to be an entrepreneur

- Define your deep-down-honest why for being an entrepreneur *so that* you have something to pull you through the tough times.

O—opportunity to define your values and success on your terms

- Identify your values *so that* you have something guiding your decisions along your journey.

- Define what success means for you *so that* you can chase it unapologetically.

U—unapologetically use what works for you

- Carve out the boundaries you need *so that* you can go after what you truly desire.

- Find your support system *so that* you have people to turn to all along the way.

- Understand your strengths and how you work best *so that* you can be more productive.

- Get clear on your finances in business *so that* you have financial confidence.

- Use ninety-day goals and progress logs *so that* you stay motivated and on track to achieving success on your terms.

Your Quarterly Check-in List:

- Are you still connected to your deep-down-honest why for being an entrepreneur?

- Are you living your core values?

- Does your definition of success still resonate with you?

- On a scale of one to five, how are you doing with each of your boundaries?

- Review your progress log to celebrate progress on your ninety-day goal.

- Set your next ninety-day goal.

As you move forward in your Accidental Entrepreneurship journey and read more books, listen to more podcasts, and work with more coaches, always check in with yourself and ask, "Does this work for me?" If the answer is yes, then go for it. If the answer is no, understand the intention behind what they are sharing and find the method that works for you.

And all along the way, I hope you hear my words in the back of your mind saying, "Be in awe of where you are." I shared the story of my first trip to New York City in the intro, and I want that to stick with you. Look up during all stages, and be in awe of where you are, even in the tough times.

You have chosen this path, and it's waiting for you. So, lace up those cute sneakers, look up in awe, then look at the path before you, and chase your success!

ACKNOWLEDGEMENTS

———

Thank you to every single person who has supported me during this writing process and my entrepreneurial journey overall.

Michael, thank you for having faith in me when I didn't yet believe in myself. Your encouragement to start my own business is the reason I am where I am today. Thank you for reminding me that I can do hard things, for listening when I need to talk, and never making me feel silly for tech meltdowns or feelings that come up. You are a pillar of strength that I know I can count on, and I'm eternally grateful for you. I love you more.

To my biz besties, my business wouldn't be the same without you, and neither would my life. I love and appreciate you all.

Shannon, thank you for listening to me, celebrating with me, and always being willing to do whatever it takes to work through business and life stuff.

Danait, thank you for embracing me as a client and then as a friend. You help me put words to my dreams and support me as I chase them.

Kendi, thank you for being the mirror I need to help me see through the fog of entrepreneurship. You help me show up unapologetically, and for that I'm so grateful.

Megan, thank you for taking a chance on me. Your confidence in me many years ago has helped me gain the courage to write this book and whatever else comes next.

Many coaches, mentors, and contractors have impacted my business, but a few people deserve special shout outs:

Mike, thank you for saying the word "unapologetic" that took me on this journey. Everyone needs a coach who believes in them like you believe in me.

Jess, thank you for taking over while I wrote this book and for all your hard work to get this book into people's hands and ears.

Cher, thank you for jumping on board to ensure that people actually know about this book and for helping me find the words to share the message.

SuZen, thank you for encouraging me to write this book over the years we've worked together. You're the best hype crew!

My book wouldn't be what you have in your hands today without the incredible help of editors.

Rachel and Anne, thank you for your patience and grace as I stumbled my way through the process of writing and editing this book. Your constant encouragement and constructive criticism allowed the book to come to life.

Eric, thank you for starting this program and for doing it your way. You and the Manuscripts team gave me the space, encouragement, and steps to write my "get-to" book instead of the "should" book. For this, I will be forever grateful.

Thank you, beta readers, for taking my draft and making it much clearer. Please know that everyone who creates a business on their terms after reading this book has you to thank: Jess, Kelli M., Katy, Pia, Alisha, Cammy, Danait, Jennifer, Kelli A., Lisa K., Lisa M., Max, Regina, and Sigrid.

And had I not started my entrepreneurial journey with the support of family and friends, my spark to help other entrepreneurs would have never been lit.

Mom, thank you for always encouraging me. I know that's where I received this gift that I now get to share with others. The ripple effect is real.

Kristie, thank you for your ride-or-die support and always making me laugh. I can't imagine life without your jokes and love.

Dale, thank you for your support and showing me the value of hard work.

Stuart, thank you for showing me that it doesn't take a business degree to have a successful business. You inspired me, and I wish I had told you this more. I miss you with my whole heart.

Karissa, thank you for your support and always reminding me that I deserve credit for my hard work. You know me well!

Dad, thank you for saying, "You won't get rich working for someone else" the moment I told you I wanted to start my own company.

Mr. Ron, thank you for being the best writing partner I could have asked for. You showed me the value of slowing down and what prioritizing really means for me.

Kelli, thank you for believing in me as an entrepreneur and author and for making this book so much better.

Mrs. Judy, David, Heather, Josh, and Brooke, thank you for supporting me. You have helped build my confidence, and I'm grateful to call you family.

Abbi, thank you for remembering my big days and texting me good luck messages.

Max, thank you for your genuine excitement and curiosity about my business.

To my nieces and nephews, I believe in you more than you can ever imagine. I love you Jada, Alanna, Eddie, Elijah, Aidan, Norah, Nathan, Malia, and Tyler.

Crystal and Katelyn, thank you for your never-wavering love and support. I love you and all your boys too.

Abbey, Bre, and Jacq, thank you for the lifelong support you give to me in everything I pursue. I love you and your families so much.

Zoe and Elsa, thank you for being at my feet through all of this and for reminding me to get up from my desk so I could take you outside and play.

A special thank you to everyone who preordered a copy of this book. You powered the publishing, and your belief in me kept me going during the hard times of writing and editing. Thank you from the bottom of my heart:

Emilie Acord, Cammy Adair, Lauren Adamo, Kelli Anders, Sue Andersen, Michael Basch, Danait Berhe, Paige Berra, Pia Burman, Meg Casebolt, Shannon Crow, Abbey Cuomo, Meg Desjarlais, Tracey Drake, Chelsea Elbert, Grace Evans, Marianna Evans, Christa Fairbrother, Cara Fitzgerald, Laura Fowler Massie, Jennifer Fultz, Dominique Gauthier, Madison George, Christie Gibertini, Carl Grant, Jessica Gulley-Ward, Cher Hale, Samantha Harrison, Mado Hesselink, Libby Hinsley, Marta Hopkins, Mikah Horn, Sarah Hunter, Tess Jewell-Larsen, Valerie Kacian, Lisa Kavanagh, Jacqueline Kelley, Marcy Kelly, Jessica Kinsey, Eric Koester, Debra Leong, Kim Lowe, Kate Lynch, Dara Madigan, SuZen Marie, Cassandra McCoy, Kelli McKinney, Max McKinney, Michael McKinney, Crystal Menzies, Lisa Meronchuk, Jeri Mills, Bre Myers, Karissa Neely, Amy Novotny, Jessica Owen, Krystie Pilens, Emmanuela Pintus, Katelyn Potter, Lauren Reek, Sue Ellen Rhine, Allison Rissel, Amy Buchan Siegfried, JR Smith, Katy Spartz, Megan Spears, Crystal Steen, Sigrid Strebe, Sarah Teague, Colleen Thakkar, Regina Trailweaver, Jani Van Grevenhof, Kendi Vrska-Weygand, Kristy West, Alisha Wielfaert, Kyle Wilkinson, Karin Wilson Edmonds, Debbie Wright, Dale Wright.

APPENDIX

―――

INTRODUCTION

Commerce Institute. 2023. "How Many New Businesses Are Started Each Year? Data Reveals the Answer." January 1, 2023.
https://www.commerceinstitute.com/new-businesses-started-every-year/.

Global Entrepreneurship Monitor. 2023. "New GEM Research: Impact of the Pandemic on Entrepreneurship Worldwide is Mixed; United Arab Emirates #1 in Global Entrepreneurship Monitor Index." Global Entrepreneurship Monitor. February 16, 2023.
https://www.gemconsortium.org/reports/latest-global-report.

Vanderbilt, Tom. 2021. "The joys of being an absolute beginner – for life." *The Guardian.* January 7, 2021.
https://www.theguardian.com/lifeandstyle/2021/jan/07/the-joys-of-being-an-absolute-beginner-for-life.

CHAPTER 2

Sinek, Simon. 2009. "Start with why — how great leaders inspire action." TEDx Talks. September 28, 2009. 18:01.
https://www.youtube.com/watch?v=u4ZoJKF_VuA.

CHAPTER 3

Caprino, Kathy. 2013. "Why Business Plans Don't Work And 'Pivoting' Is Nonsense." *Forbes.* March 5, 2013.
https://www.forbes.com/sites/kathycaprino/2013/03/05/why-business-plans-dont-work-and-pivoting-is-nonsense.

Co-Active Training Institute. n.d. "Co-Active Coaching Toolkit." Accessed September 7, 2022.
https://coactive.com/resources/coaching-toolkit-registration.

Miller, Nathan. 2022. "Want Success? Define Your Company Values." *Entrepreneur.* July 28, 2022. https://www.entrepreneur.com/starting-a-business/defining-your-companys-values-will-transform-your-company/430326.

Transcend. 2022. "How Workplace Values Impact Decision Making, Behavior, and Communication in the Workplace." April 27, 2022. https://transcendbusiness.com/team-leadership/how-workplace-values-impact-decision-making-behavior-and-communication-in-the-workplace/.

CHAPTER 4

Benisek, Alexandra. 2022. "What Is Imposter Syndrome?" WebMD. February 15, 2022. https://www.webmd.com/balance/what-is-imposter-syndrome.

DOIT. "Mentor Tip: Definition of Success." University of Washington. Accessed August 19, 2022. https://www.washington.edu/doit/mentor-tip-definition-success.

McKinney, Amanda. 2020. "You've Got This! Yoga Business Pep Talk From Amanda." *The Unapologetic Entrepreneur.* Released March 30, 2020. Podcast, 14 min. https://www.amandamckinney.com/post/episode39.

Talbot, Jo. "10 Successful People Who've Had Imposter Syndrome." Humanest. May 4, 2021. https://humanestcare.com/self-help/blog/10-successful-people-whove-had-imposter-syndrome.

CHAPTER 5

Economist. 1955. "Parkinson's Law." Accessed September 10, 2022. https://www.economist.com/news/1955/11/19/parkinsons-law.

Good Therapy. 2017. "Boundaries." June 27, 2017. https://www.goodtherapy.org/blog/psychpedia/boundaries.

KuneoDallas. 2013. "Whiteboard Explainer: The Playground Study." KuneoDallas. July 16, 2013. 2:07. https://www.youtube.com/watch?v=8O8hHYIMHuo.

Burman, Pia, and Amanda McKinney. 2022. "Mindset Series: Find Balance Using The 8+8+8 Framework." *The Unapologetic Entrepreneur.* Released May 30, 2022. Podcast, 51 min. https://www.amandamckinney.com/post/mindset-series-find-balance-using-888-framework.

Sanfilippo. 2023. "How to Improve Your Work-Life Balance Today." *Business News Daily.* January 23, 2023. https://www.businessnewsdaily.com/5244-improve-work-life-balance-today.html.

Tawwab, Nedra Glover. 2016. *Set Boundaries Find Peace: A Guide To Reclaiming Yourself.* New York City: TarcherPerigee.

CHAPTER 6

Carter, Timothy. 2021. "The True Failure Rate of Small Businesses." *Entrepreneur.* January 3, 2021. https://www.entrepreneur.com/starting-a-business/the-true-failure-rate-of-small-businesses/361350.

Koester, Eric, and Adam Saven. 2022. *Super Mentors.* Washington, DC: New Degree Press.

MasterClass. 2021. "How to Succeed in Business: 5 Strategies for Entrepreneurs." December 15, 2021. https://www.masterclass.com/articles/how-to-succeed-in-business-5-strategies-for-entrepreneurs#6lq6nxnlFKwOvfa5hfX5wI.

McKinney, Amanda. 2021. "Feeling defeated? This episode's for you [how I navigated a tech-tough day]." *The Unapologetic Entrepreneur.* Released February 8, 2021. Podcast, 27 min.

Williams, Nick. 2020. "The importance of emotional support for entrepreneurs in a crisis." Leeds University: Centre for Enterprise and Entrepreneurship Studies. September 21, 2020. https://business.leeds.ac.uk/cees/dir-record/research-blog/1758/the-importance-of-emotional-support-for-entrepreneurs-in-a-crisis.

de Witte, Melissa. 2022. "Asking for help is hard, but people want to help more than we realize, Stanford scholar says." *Stanford News.* September 8, 2022. https://news.stanford.edu/2022/09/08/asking-help-hard-people-want-help-realize/.

Wynnberg, Wilbert. 2020. "10 Tips For Becoming A Successful Entrepreneur." *Forbes.* December 28, 2020. https://www.forbes.com/sites/forbesbusinesscouncil/2021/12/28/10-tips-for-becoming-a-successful-entrepreneur/?sh=9b41c483f244.

CHAPTER 7

Basyah, Jihan. 2022. "The 3 Biggest Reasons So Many People Love To Take Personality Tests." Well + Good. June 15, 2022. https://www.wellandgood.com/why-use-personality-tests/.

Cherry, Kendra. 2022. "How the Myers-Briggs Type Indicator Works." VeryWell Mind. July 28, 2022. https://www.verywellmind.com/the-myers-briggs-type-indicator-2795583.

Gallup. 2023. CliftonStrengths. Accessed February 17, 2023. https://www.gallup.com/cliftonstrengths/en/253676/how-cliftonstrengths-works.aspx.

Harper, Heather. 2023. "The 23 Best Personality Tests In Ranking Order (2023 Update)." Workstyle. July 3, 2018. https://www.workstyle.io/best-personality-test.

Human Design. n.d. "What is the Human Design System?" My Body Graph.
Accessed September 4, 2022.
https://www.mybodygraph.com/what-is-the-human-design-system.

Johns Hopkins. n.d. "Ayurveda." Accessed September 4, 2022.
https://www.hopkinsmedicine.org/health/wellness-and-prevention/.

Joyce, Caneel. 2021. "What is your Zone of Genius?" *Caneel* (blog) on Medium.
January 12, 2021.
https://caneel.medium.com/what-is-your-zone-of-genius-58dfc8bbd4f7.

Kolbe Corp. n.d. "KOLBE A™ INDEX." Accessed September 4, 2022.
https://www.kolbe.com/kolbe-a-index/.

McCord, Beth. 2019. "Breaking Down the Enneagram." Your Enneagram Coach.
January 6, 2019.
https://www.yourenneagramcoach.com/blog/breaking-down-the-enneagram.

Michalowitz, Mike, and Amanda McKinney. 2021. "Mike Michalowicz: Creating
Healthy Money Habits Through Profit First." *The Unapologetic Entrepreneur.*
Released June 14, 2021. Podcast, 33 min.

CHAPTER 8

Michalowicz, Mike. 2017. *Profit First.* New York: Portfolio.

Sincero, Jen. 2017. *You Are A Badass At Making Money: Master The Mindset Of
Wealth.* New York: Penguin Life.

CHAPTER 9

American Psychological Association. 2015. "Frequently monitoring progress toward
goals increases chance of success." *Science Daily.* October 29, 2015.
https://www.sciencedaily.com/releases/2015/10/151029101349.htm.

Brown, Damon. 2019. "This Perfect Bill Gates Quote Will Frame Your Next Decade."
Inc. December 4, 2019.
https://www.inc.com/damon-brown/this-perfect-bill-gates-quote-will-frame-your-
next-decade-of-success.html.

Loucadoux, Michelle. 2021. "Day Tracking Can Reveal the Truth about Your
Productivity." Medium. October 13, 2021.
https://betterhumans.pub/day-tracking-can-reveal-the-truth-about-your-
productivity-57093ae74596.

Merriam-Webster. 2023. "Goal." Accessed October 2, 2022.
https://www.merriam-webster.com/dictionary/goal.

McKinney, Amanda. 2022. "The ONE thing that has helped me succeed in business."
The Unapologetic Entrepreneur. Released January 10, 2022. Podcast, 31 min.

Morwitz, Vicci G., and Gavan J. Fitzsimons. 2008. "The Mere-Measurement Effect: Why Does Measuring Intentions Change Actual Behavior?" *Journal Of Consumer Psychology.* https://myscp.onlinelibrary.wiley.com/doi/10.1207/s15327663jcp1401%262_8.

Robbins, Mel. 2017. "The Secret to Stopping Fear and Anxiety (That Actually Works)." Mel Robbins. February 8, 2017. 12:00. https://www.youtube.com/watch?v=6n8i7uaomSw.

Made in the USA
Middletown, DE
14 July 2023

35177788R00099